International Phonetic Alphabet

for

Singers

A manual for English and Foreign Language Diction

Joan Wall

Pst... Inc
Dallas, Texas

ISBN 1-877761-50-8

Printed in the United States of America

Copies of this book may be ordered by contacting:

Pst ... Inc.
P.O. Box 800208H
Dallas, Texas 75380-0208

Edited by Robert Caldwell
Cover design: Marti Dees
Graphic Artist: Ernie Ludwick

10-9-8-7-6-5-4

Second Printing

Table Of Contents

PART I: INTRODUCTION TO THE INTERNATIONAL PHONETIC ALPHABET

PART II: VOWELS

CHAPTER 1
THE CONTENT
AND VALUE
OF THE
INTERNATIONAL
PHONETIC ALPHABET

What are Phonetics?

The study of phonetics is the study of speech sounds. Or, more precisely, it is the study of the symbols which *represent* speech sounds. A phonetic alphabet is an alphabet in which a *single* sound is represented by a *single* symbol. The International Phonetic Alphabet, or IPA, is such an alphabet.

A quick look at the roman alphabet of English will show that it is certainly not a phonetic alphabet, that sound and spelling are often not the same.

For example, the sound of *ee* may have seven different spellings:

be eat beet receive people brief Phoenix.

A single symbol may stand for many sounds. For example, look at the different sounds that can come from the ninth letter of the alphabet, *i* :

ah-ih in might	*ee* in liter
ih in mitt	*sh* in nation.

A single letter may not have a sound at all, such as the *p* in *pneunomia*. Still other letters represent more than one sound, as in the word *mix* where the letter *x* has two sounds: *ks*. Two words may also be spelled differently, but pronounced alike: *peace* and *piece*.

Americans are sometimes unaware of the sounds of their own language and often confuse the letters of the alphabet with the sounds of the language. For instance, when asked how many vowel sounds are in English, they will likely answer five vowels—meaning the five letters of the alphabet, a-e-i-o-u. Yet, in English there are actually *twenty-two* vowel sounds, sixteen pure vowel sounds and six diphthongs! The list below shows all twenty-two vowel sounds and how each sound has its own unique IPA symbol.

*A **pure vowel** sound consists of only one distinct vowel sound; a **diphthong** is a distinct vowel unit made up of two pure vowel sounds.*

Figure 1: The IPA symbols for English vowels.

IPA Symbols in General American Dialect

Pure Vowels

Forward Vowels:	[i]	b**ee**t	
	[ɪ]	b**i**t	
	[e]	ch**a**otic	(pure [e] seldom used)
	[ɛ]	b**e**t	
	[æ]	b**a**t	
	[a]	*bright ah*	(used mostly in diphthongs)

aisle

Back Vowels:	[u]	b**oo**t	
	[ʊ]	b**oo**k	
	[o]	**o**bey	(pure [o] seldom used)
	[ɔ]	s**aw**	
	[ɑ]	**ah**	*father*

Central Vowels:	[ʌ]	**u**p	*(stressed uh)*
	[ə]	**a**bout	*(unstressed uh, schwa)*
	[ɜ]	h**er**d	*(stressed, r-colored vowel)*
	[ɜ]	h**er**d	*(not r-colored)*
	[ɚ]	butt**er**	*(unstressed, r-colored vowel)*

Diphthongs

	[eɪ]	b**ai**t
	[oʊ]	b**oa**t
	[aɪ]	b**i**te
	[aʊ]	**ou**ch
	[ɔɪ]	b**oy**
	[ju]	**u**se

What is the International Phonetic Alphabet?

The International Phonetic Alphabet (IPA) is a true phonetic alphabet in which *one* symbol stands for *one* sound. And with remarkably few modifications, today this alphabet remains as it was when established by the International Phonetic Association in 1886.

Many of the IPA symbols are the same as the letters in our roman alphabet, which makes the IPA easy to learn. In fact, sixteen of the English letters are identical to the symbols of the IPA. This leaves only nine new consonant symbols and sixteen pure vowel symbols to be learned.

IPA symbols are recognized by their enclosure in brackets. For example, the symbol for the sound of *b* as in the word *boy* is [b]; the symbol for the vowel sound of *ee* as in *bee* is [i]; and the symbol for *t* as in *tea* is [t]. Therefore, the symbols representing the word *beet* are [bit].

The process of using only one symbol per sound promotes easy and accurate communication about speech sounds. Because the IPA is a universal alphabet, IPA symbols are used to transcribe words in foreign languages, such as Italian, French, German, Spanish or Latin. This symbol consistency in multiple languages is very helpful to singers who are required to sing in languages other than their own.

The Value of the IPA

The study of the International Phonetic Alphabet is valuable to singers for several reasons.

English and foreign language diction books and dictionaries use IPA to communicate pronunciations.

Foreign language diction texts used in music departments of universities, for example, use IPA as a common language to communicate pronunciation rules. Being able to read the IPA allows the student to take better advantage of these beneficial Italian, French, and German diction texts.

Phonetic Readings of Songs and Arias by Coffin, Errolle, Singer and DeLattre, a reference work used frequently in diction courses and in private voice studios, contains transcriptions of

Italian, German, and French art songs and arias. This book is a dependable source for correct pronunciations of words in foreign language songs, but it requires the singer to have good facility with the IPA.

Figure 2: Sample of IPA transcription in Phonetic Readings of Songs and Arias.

```
Schubert    Der Wanderer
            der vandərər

Ich komme vom Gebirge her,
ɪç kɔmmə fɔm gəbɪrgə heːr,

es dampft das Tal, es braust das Meer.
ɛs dampft das tɑːl, ɛs brɑost das meːr.
```

Several contemporary foreign language dictionaries, such as The Bantam New College French and English Dictionary, include IPA transcriptions of words. Precise pronunciations are communicated to the reader.

A significant reference work for English pronunciations is A Pronouncing Dictionary of American English by Kenyon and Knott. Its IPA transcriptions of words clarify the standard pronunciations of English words in General American diction as well as in regional dialects. This dictionary answers questions about English pronunciations in a more definitive way than the sometimes confusing old stand-by, Webster's Dictionary.

Figure 3: Sample of IPA transcriptions in A Pronouncing Dictionary of American English.

B

B, b *letter* **bi** |*pl* B's, Bs, *poss* B's **biz**
baa **bæː, baː; bɑː** |*3 sg* baaes, *pl n* baas **-z** |-ed **-d** |-ing **-ɪŋ**
Baal **ˈbeəl, bel**
babbitt, B- **ˈbæbɪt** |-ed **-ɪd**
babble **ˈbæbḷ** |-d **-d** |-ling **ˈbæbḷɪŋ, -blɪŋ**
babe **beb**
Babel **ˈbebḷ, ˈbæbḷ**
Bab el Mandeb **ˈbæbˌɛlˈmændɛb, ˈbɑbˌɛlˈman-**
baboo, babu **ˈbɑbu**

Bacheller **ˈbætʃələ˞, ˈbætʃlə˞; ES -lə(r**
bachelor **ˈbætʃələ˞, ˈbætʃlə˞; ES -lə(r**
Bachman **ˈbækmən, bɑk- (***Ger* **ˈbɑxmɑn)**
bacillary **ˈbæsḷˌɛrɪ, ˈbæsɪˌl-**
bacillus **bəˈsɪləs** |-li **-laɪ**
back **bæk** |-ed **-t** |-ache **-ˌek**
backbite **ˈbækˌbaɪt** |-bit **-ˌbɪt** |-bitten **-ˌbɪtṇ**
backbone **ˈbækˌbon, -ˌbon** |-d **-d**
backfire *n* **ˈbækˌfaɪr; ES -ˌfaɪə(r**
backfire *v* **ˈbækˌfaɪr, -ˈfaɪr; ES -aɪə(r; |-d -d**
backgammon **ˈbækˌgæmən, ˌbækˈgæmən**

Current vocal pedagogy texts and vocal research studies use IPA symbols.

Today's vocal pedagogy texts and vocal research studies generously use IPA symbols, as the samples on the next page indicate. IPA knowledge supports the singer who wishes to stay abreast of the latest vocal research and pedagogical ideas.

Figure 4: Examples from The Structure of Singing, by Richard Miller.

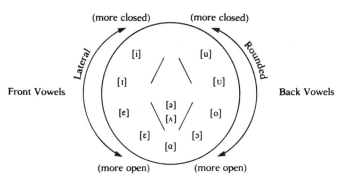

Figure 11.1. Vowel Modification *(aggiustamento)* Chart

Figure 5: Sample from the NATS Bulletin. (Jan/Feb 1985 Jeffrey Foote)

Vowels need modification in the *upper registers especially* in order to achieve head voice. The [i] should become [y] (the umlaut ü); [e] becomes [œ]; [a] becomes mixed with [ʌ] and [ʊ] ; [o] becomes mixed with [u] and [ʊ] . These modifications help to maintain the speaking (lower) formant in the tone as the pitch raises; as the formants present become higher and higher, tone tends to become shrill, screechy and pinched in women and yelly and strident in men.

Figure 7: Sample from The Overtones of Bel Canto by Berton Coffin.

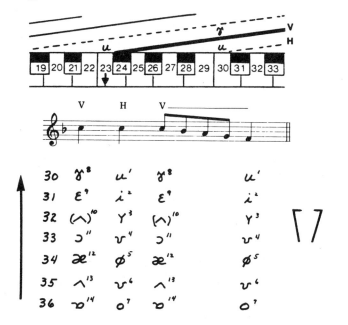

Figure 6: Example from The Science of the Singing Voice by Johan Sundberg.

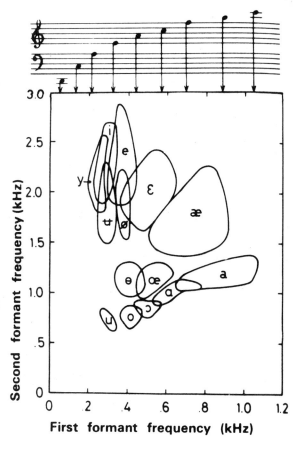

***IPA offers a positive influence on the development of the
singing tone.***

The old masters of voice teaching have said: *Chi sa ben
respirare e sillabare, sapra ben cantare,* meaning if you breathe and
articulate well, you will sing well. The concept of building a singing
technic upon the clear and easy articulation of speech sounds is
certainly not new. Traditionally, singers have spent considerable time
rehearsing accurate vowel production, articulation and diction to
develop a desirable tonal quality.

Precise vowel enunciation, along with good breath
management, forms the primary foundation for the control of good
tonal production and enables a singer to sing with sonority, beauty,
flexibility and expressiveness. And, of course, distinct articulation
enhances communication of lyrics and artistic shaping of musical
phrases.

This text proposes that by anchoring speech sounds to
specific phonetic symbols, concepts of articulation and tonal
production are strengthened. As a single sound is attached or
anchored to a single symbol, the memory of that sound and its
physical method of production becomes more accurate and secure.
This has been found true, not only with beginning singers, but even
with advanced university students, who discover their singing
improves after learning IPA in diction courses. They hear the vowels
better. They can respond more quickly to suggestions about tone
color. Resonance improves.

***The use of IPA results in more precise communication about
speech sounds and pronunciations.***

As sounds become associated with a specific visual
symbol, communication between teacher and student (or author and
reader) can become more precise. A teacher can write the symbol as
it is spoken. Flash cards or posters can also assist communication
and learning. When students see the symbol as well as hear the
sound, they can more clearly understand the difference between
confusing sounds; for example, the vowel sounds in such words as
pin [pɪn] and *pen* [pɛn] or *marry* [mærɪ] and *merry* [mɛrɪ].

Intended Use

The <u>International</u> <u>Phonetic</u> <u>Alphabet</u> <u>for</u> <u>Singers</u> is intended to be used as a text for language diction and vocal pedagogy courses, as supplementary material in the private studio or with choirs, and by any individual who wishes to learn or brush-up on IPA. This workbook is a training manual written specifically for singers to learn the symbols, sounds and transcriptions of the basic IPA.

Each chapter contains descriptive comments about individual language sounds, how they are physically produced, their major characteristics, and common problems. The exercises guide accurate articulation and develop the ability to write and read IPA transcriptions of English words. In addition, there are exercises that use IPA transcriptions of nonsense words to build skill for reading IPA transcriptions of foreign languages. There is a special section devoted to additional IPA symbols for Italian, French and German.

The symbols are presented progressively. Only symbols which have been studied previously are used in subsequent chapters. It is important to use the material in the order presented.

A word of caution: people in different parts of the United States pronounce words and individual speech sounds differently. Therefore, if you are studying this material outside of class, find someone knowledgeable in IPA who can clarify the sounds of each symbol. A teacher is always the best guide. Once secure in the sounds of the symbols, an individual can study the basic IPA from this manual and gain skills in reading and transcribing the IPA.

Conclusion

Speech sounds form the basis of vocal technic and art. Knowledge of IPA helps the singer use foreign language diction texts, English and foreign language dictionaries, pedagogy texts, and research studies. By anchoring symbol and sound, the IPA offers a positive, controlling influence on the development of the singing tone. Communication between teacher and student is enhanced and, finally, the few symbols of IPA are easy to learn.

CHAPTER 2
HELPFUL HINTS
FOR USING
THE IPA

This chapter will offer a few helpful hints and definitions so you can learn the International Phonetic Alphabet more easily.

Brackets: IPA symbols are placed in brackets and are called symbols to distinguish them from the letters of the English alphabet.

[t] is an IPA symbol.

Letters and symbols: The letters of the alphabet of a language are referred to as orthographic letters, which distinguishes them from IPA symbols.

t is an orthographic letter.

till is an orthographic spelling.

[t] is an IPA symbol.

[tɪl] is an IPA spelling or transcription.

Names of symbols: An IPA symbol is normally referred to by its sound. There are a few symbols which have special names and these will be noted in the appropriate chapter.

The symbol [i] is called by its sound *ee* .

The [t] is called by its sound *t.*

Transcribing: Writing a word in IPA symbols is called spelling or transcribing the word. When writing in IPA symbols, be sure to transcribe the sounds within a word and not the orthographic letters. Some common pitfalls to avoid are listed below. Do not be concerned at this point that you cannot read the IPA symbols given in these examples. Just let yourself become familiar with the principles being described.

Silent letters: Do not transcribe silent letters into IPA.

> *know* is [noʊ], without the *k*.

> *psalm* is [sɑm], without the *p* or *l*.

Double letters: Transcribe only what your hear. Double letters do not sound different from single letters, so transcribe the single sound with a single IPA symbol.

> *bell* is [bɛl], with only one *l*.

> *mess* is [mɛs], with only one *s*.

Capital letters: IPA symbols remain the same whether or not the orthographic word being transcribed is capitalized.

> *Francis* would be ['fræn sɪs].

> *Bob* would be [bɑb].

Punctuation: Do not use apostrophe marks in IPA.

> *Pete's* is [pits]

> *school's* is [skulz]

Penmanship: Take care in writing the symbols. Several IPA symbols look similar and can be easily confused if written carelessly.

> *schwa* [ə] can look like *ah* [ɑ].

> *th* [ð] can look like *ûr* [ɚ].

> *sh* [ʃ] can look like capital *S*.

> Write [l] with a looped stroke. Without a loop, handwritten [|] tends to look like the vertical line of the symbol for a pause [|].

Accent Marks for Syllabic Stress

Stressing individual syllables is one of the major elements that gives language its rhythm and flow. It is achieved by changing the loudness, duration, pitch, and vowel choice of the syllable. Stress must be carefully observed for language to be easily understood and words correctly pronounced. In English there are primary, secondary and unstressed syllables.

In IPA, small marks are used to show where the stress falls within the word. The mark which indicates the primary stress is placed above and before the syllable. In the following words, the underlined syllable is the one with primary stress.

> *reason* would transcribe as ['ri zən].

> *discuss* would transcribe as [dɪs 'kʌs].

In some two-syllable words, there is equal primary stress.

handmade would be [ˈhænd ˈmeɪd].

bookcase would be [ˈbʊk ˈkeɪs].

Words which have two or more syllables often include a syllable with secondary stress. The secondary stress is indicated with the accent mark below the line and before the syllable. In the following words, the underlined syllables are the ones with secondary stress.

stair<u>case</u> would be [ˈstɛr ˌkeɪs].

foot<u>ball</u> would be [ˈfʊt ˌbɔl].

Unstressed syllables do not need an accent mark. Unstressing in English is indicated by the weakening of the sound of the vowel to a more neutral sound such as *uh* [ə] or another shortened vowel. In the following words, the underlined syllables are unstressed.

di<u>ffer</u> would transcribe as [ˈdɪ fər].

<u>a</u>loud would transcribe as [ə ˈlaʊd].

pois<u>on</u> would transcribe as [ˈpɔɪ zən].

One-syllable words do not need accent marks.

wood would be [wʊd].

tin would be [tɪn].

Here is a simple trick that can make reading stress in words easier for the beginning IPA student. Create a nonsense word which captures only the accented rhythm of the word. For instance, in the word *about* the second syllable has the strongest stress, so you might say da-DUM. You can say the rhythm of any word by indicating the primary stress with a louder sound, such as da-DUM, DUM-dee, or dee-DUM-dee, without being concerned about the pronunciation of the word. In the word [ˈoʊ pən] you would say DUM-dee because the first syllable has the primary stress. Try this in the following examples. Read aloud and indicate on the stress in these words.

[kən ˈdʌkt] dee-DUM

[ˌkɑn ˈkeɪv] dee-DUM

[ˈstʌ dɪ] DUM-dee

[ɪn ˈfɔr məl] dee-DUM-dee

[ˌɑr ˈtɪ kjə ˌleɪt] dee-DUM-dee-dah

Phonemes and Allophones

A phoneme ['foʊ ˌnim] is a single language sound that is represented by a single symbol, and is the smallest speech unit in IPA. The phoneme [t], for example, indicates a sound of the *t* in the word *team*.

Within each phoneme, however, there may be slight variations of the pronunciation even though the identity of the particular sound is still maintained. For example, the [t] in the word *team* is produced with the tip of the tongue placed more forward in the mouth than when saying the [t] in the word *wart*. Yet, in both cases the identity of the sound is maintained, allowing it to be easily recognizable as [t], even though the sound of each [t] is slightly different. These slight variations in the pronunciations of the same sound are called allophones ['æ lə ˌfoʊnz]. Foreign languages include many such variations and singers will learn these allophones when they study the language.

*A **phoneme** is an individual language sound and an **allophone** is any slight variation within that same sound.*

Phonetic Transcriptions

When reading IPA transcriptions from different sources, you will discover that authors rarely agree completely on IPA spellings. Each author can use the IPA to suit any number of individual purposes — to accurately depict the general dialect, or a specific regional dialect, or some other distinctive use. This author, for example, has transcribed words specifically to help the singer. For example, the pronunciation of stressed *ûr* [ɝ] and unstressed *ûr* [ɚ] requires the retraction of the tongue, which is not conducive to vocal freedom on sustained singing tones. So, instead, this author transcribes *ûr* sounds as [ɜr] and [ər], which is much more conducive to singing. This is further discussed in Chapter 6: The Central Vowels.

Stressing and unstressing will be fully discussed in Chapter 6

Another special consideration for singers is the spelling of syllabic consonants, which occurs in words like *little*, *bottle*, or *able*. In these words, the *le* is heard as a syllabized or vowelized *l*. The *l* actually becomes a syllable and is sustained as a vowel. However, on long sustained notes, the syllabic *l* [l̩] cannot produce a substantial singing tone. Therefore, singers sing the word *little* as *lit-uhl* ['lɪ təl]. So the IPA transcription of *le* in this text is [əl], though in most speech IPA texts it is spelled with a dot underneath: [l̩]

little ['lɪ təl]

bottle ['bɑ təl]

fiddle ['fɪ dəl]

settle ['sɛ təl]

Conclusion

Remember, the most important value of IPA is that it breaks down all the complex sounds of languages into individual units, and attaches a symbol to each one. By naming and classifying these isolated sounds, singers can more accurately thread together the string of sounds they choose to sing. If there is a question about the correct pronunciation, refer to a dictionary when doing the exercises in this book.

Be sure to speak the words aloud. Linger over the sounds, caress them, savour them, enjoy them. Feel the movements of your tongue, lips and jaw as you go from one sound to another. Listen carefully to your pronunciation and articulation. These exercises will provide the opportunity for you to become intimately aware of your articulation, a must for singing diction.

CHAPTER 3
INTRODUCTION TO
VOWELS

Classification of Speech Sounds

Every speech sound has distinctive characteristics which become the basis of language classification. The various sounds of the IPA symbols are classified by the position and movements of the articulators (the tongue, lips, jaw, and soft palate). See Figure 8 to familiarize yourself with the names of the parts of the oral cavity.

For the purpose of study and communication, language sounds are grouped into two primary speech classifications: vowels and consonants.

Consonants are speech sounds which have some type of interference or interruption of the air stream as it moves through the vocal tract (the throat, mouth, and nose). Consonants will be discussed fully in Chapters 8-14.

Vowels are speech sounds which are produced without any major interruption of the air flow through the vocal tract. In other words, the articulators do not touch· each other or cause any obstruction in the air flow.

Each time we move the tongue around in the mouth or change the position of the lips or jaw, we change the acoustic properties of the vocal tract. The slight differences in the resonance frequencies of the vocal tract produce the sounds we identify as vowels.

Figure 8: The Oral Cavity and Its Articulators

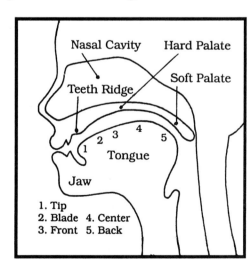

1. Tip
2. Blade 4. Center
3. Front 5. Back

Figure 9: Diagram of tongue positions for certain vowels.

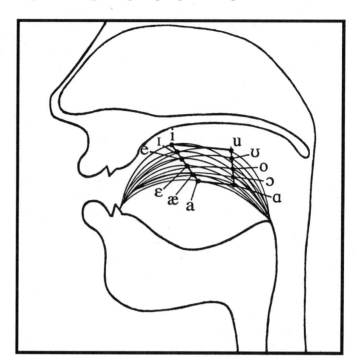

Classification of Vowels

A vowel is called a *pure* vowel when its sound can be sustained without movement of the articulators or any change in the quality of sound until the air flow ceases. In English, there are sixteen pure vowel sounds. Vowels will be presented fully in Chapters 4 through 7.

A *diphthong* is a vowel unit made up of two pure vowels with the acoustic result being perceived as a single distinguishable unit. In English there are six diphthongs. Diphthongs are fully discussed in Chapter 7.

Vowels are further grouped into classifications determined by the positioning of the tongue, lips and jaw. These include 1) forward, back and central vowels, 2) close, mid or open vowels, and 3) rounded or unrounded vowels.

For all sung vowels, the tongue tip remains touching the back of the bottom front teeth while the body of the tongue, the lips, and jaw move around to create the various vowel sounds. See Figure 9 to observe the positions of the tongue for forward and back vowels.

Figure 10: The Vowel Diagram

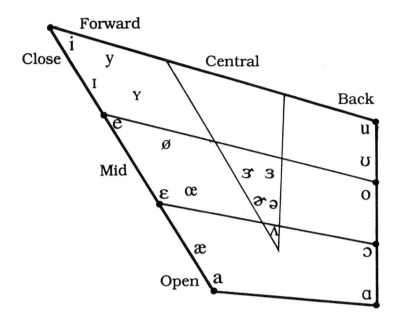

The shape of the Vowel Diagram in Figure 10 can also be seen in Figure 9 by observing the dark line connecting the dots which represent the high point of the arch of the tongue for each vowel.

The spacial relationship of vowels to each other can be explained by means of a diagram such as the one in Figure 10. Its approximate present form came from Daniel Jones of University College, London, and is known as the Vowel Diagram. It was developed by superimposing X-ray images of the position of the tongue when articulating various vowels. The Vowel Diagram, Figure 10, indicates the position of the high point of the tongue during the articulation of each vowel.

On the Vowel Diagram, the terms *forward, central* and *back* refer to whether the arch of the tongue is forward, central or back in the mouth. *Close, mid* and *open* refer to the width of the the space between the tongue and the roof of the mouth. The closer the tongue to the roof, the more close the vowel. The more open the space and more dropped the jaw, the more open the vowel.

The terms *rounding* and *unrounding* refer to the position of the lips. Most back vowels use rounded lips, while forward vowels are produced with unrounded lips.

In Figures 9 and 10, *ee* [i] can be seen to be a *close, forward* vowel, which means that the high point of the arch of the tongue is close to the roof of the mouth and forward in the mouth. On the other hand, *ōō* [u] is considered a *high, back* vowel because the arch of the tongue is high and back in the mouth. Note that for *ōō* [u] the lips are rounded. *Ah* [ɑ] is a *low back* vowel because the tongue is low in the mouth.

CHAPTER 4
FORWARD VOWELS

Introduction to Forward Vowels

The teeth ridge is also called the **alveolar** [ˌæl ˈvi ə lɚ] **ridge,** *and the soft palate may be called the* **velum.**

The forward vowels are those produced with the arch of the tongue *forward* in the mouth, near the teeth ridge or hard palate. For each forward vowel, the tip of the tongue touches the back of the bottom front teeth. The lips are in a neutral position, neither spread nor rounded. The soft palate is raised, closing off the nasal passage. The forward vowels of English are:

[i] as in b<u>ee</u>t.
[ɪ] as in b<u>i</u>t.
[eɪ] as in b<u>ai</u>t.
[ɛ] as in b<u>e</u>t.
[æ] as in b<u>a</u>t.
[a] as in B<u>o</u>ston (as spoken by New Englanders).

In singing and in speech, vowels are essentially produced the same. Forward vowels are characterized by the arch of the tongue being forward in the mouth. One difference might be noted. In singing, the jaw is often lower than in speech. When the jaw lowers, the tongue needs to move more forward in the mouth to maintain the vowel integrity.

Another difference between speech and singing which sometimes occurs, involves the position of the soft palate. In speech, the soft palate is raised, closing the passageway to the nose, on all sounds except *m*, *n*, and *ng*. In singing, however, the position of the soft palate is debated among pedagogues. Some teachers believe the soft palate should be raised at all times. Other teachers believe it should be raised some times and lowered at others. In the following descriptions of vowels, the position of the soft palate follows the speech position. The teacher or student may adjust the position as desired for singing.

A. Practice the sounds of these forward vowels.

Read aloud the following words.

[i]	[ɪ]
beet	bit
meet	mitt
geese	give
keen	king
deed	did
team	tin

Contrast the sounds of the various forward vowels. Become familiar with the IPA symbol which represents each sound.

[ɪ]	[ɛ]
bit	bet
give	get
mid	met
pin	pen
bin	Ben
tin	ten

*Sometimes the word **get** [gɛt] is mispronounced **git** [gɪt]. Become aware of the subtle differences in sound between each forward vowel.*

[ɪ]	[ɛ]	[æ]
bit	bet	bat
pin	pen	pan
sin	send	sand
mere	merry	marry
tin	ten	tan

[i]	[ɪ]	[ɛ]	[æ]
beet	bit	bet	bat
seat	sit	set	sat
heed	hid	head	had

Diphthongal [eɪ] is consistently used in American English in place of pure [e] (See Chapter 4 Exercises)

[i]	[ɪ]	[eɪ]	[ɛ]	[æ]
beet	bit	bait	bet	bat
meet	mitt	mate	met	mat
Dean	din	dane	den	Dan

[i]

[ɪ]

[e]

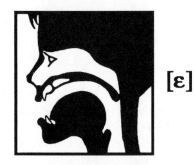

[ɛ]

[æ]

Whisper the following list of vowels several times.

Whisper *ee*	**[i]**	(*as in b<u>ee</u>t*)
Whisper *ih*	**[ɪ]**	(*as in b<u>i</u>t*)
Whisper *ay*	**[eɪ]**	(*as in b<u>ai</u>t*)
Whisper *eh*	**[ɛ]**	(*as in b<u>e</u>t*)
Whisper *ă*	**[æ]**	(*as in b<u>a</u>t*)

As you whisper, keep your throat and jaw as relaxed as possible and be careful not to use a guttural attack. The tip of your tongue should be gently touching the back of the bottom teeth for each vowel sound.

Whisper the list of vowels again. Notice that several changes will occur in the size and shape of your mouth as you proceed down the list from **[i]** to **[æ]**. First, your jaw progressively lowers and the space between the tongue and palate becomes more open as you read from **[i]** to **[æ]**. For **[i]** the space between the tongue and palate is quite small, no larger than the point of a pencil. For **[æ]** your jaw is dropped to a lower position and the space between the tongue and the palate is more open.

You might find it helpful to look in a mirror and see the changes take place. The positions of the tongue, jaw and lips during the production of each of the forward vowels are also illustrated in the diagrams on the left.

Also notice that for **[i ɪ eɪ ɛ]**, the side edges of the tongue have lateral contact with the upper molars. For the fifth vowel **[æ]**, the jaw is dropped considerably and the tongue may or may not be touching the back upper molars, depending upon your personal articulation habits. For a more resonant singing tone, it is often helpful to sing **[æ]** without lateral contact of the tongue with the side molars.

Transfer the ease and clarity of the whispered vowels into speech.

After whispering *ee* [i] several times, then speak *ee* [i] several times on a pitch in your normal speaking range. Do not change the vowel sound nor the physical shape of the vowel when transferring from whispering to speaking. Maintain a relaxed jaw and throat. Repeat the same process for each vowel.

Whisper [i i i],   speak [i i i]   (as in b*ee*t).
Whisper [ɪ ɪ ɪ],   speak [ɪ ɪ ɪ]   (as in b*i*t).
Whisper [eɪ eɪ eɪ], speak [eɪ eɪ eɪ] (as in b*ai*t).
Whisper [ɛ ɛ ɛ],   speak [ɛ ɛ ɛ]   (as in b*e*t).
Whisper [æ æ æ],   speak [æ æ æ]   (as in b*a*t).

In the IPA, there is a sixth forward vowel, the *bright ah* [a], which is rarely used in its pure form in English. In our language [a] occurs primarily in the New England dialect (as in *pahk the cahr* for *park the car*) or in diphthongs (as in the word *by* [baɪ]). The pure *bright ah* [a], however, is generously used in foreign languages. This sound will be fully discussed in Chapter 4 Exercises.

Exercises

The forward vowel [i] as in b<u>ee</u>t

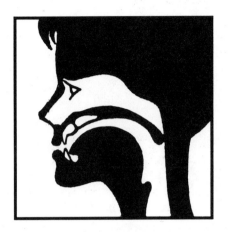

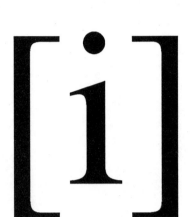

Description

Tongue

The high point of the tongue is forward in the mouth, close to the teeth ridge, which makes [i] a close, forward vowel. The tip of the tongue touches the back of the bottom front teeth. The sides of the tongue laterally touch the inside of the upper molars.

Jaw

Relaxed.

Lips

Gently parted, unrounded.

Soft Palate

Raised, closing off the nasal passageway.

Common Problems

The substitution of [i] for [ɪ] as in *keeng* for *king*

Drawing the lips back into a smile. Although [i] can be produced this way, it is not necessary. All that is necessary to produce the clear [i] is the raised forward position of the tongue.

When [l] follows [i] in the same syllable, there is sometimes a tendency to add *uh* [ə]. *Feel* becomes *fee-uhl* [fiəl].

A. *Practice the* [i] *sound.*

Read aloud these sounds.

[bi] (*as in* <u>bee</u>), [bi], [bi], [bi], [bi]

[pi] (*as in* <u>pea</u>), [pi], [pi], [pi], [pi]

[ib], [ip], [ib], [ip]

Read aloud these English words using [i].

[bit], [bid], [bim], [biz]

Caution: Be sure to pronounce these words with the [i] sound as in *beet* and not [ɪ] as in *bit.*

[bit]	=	beet
[bid]	=	bead
[bim]	=	beam
[biz]	=	bees

Read aloud these nonsense words using [i].

[id], [im], [ig], [if]

Read aloud these pairs of words.

Caution: Be careful not to drawl your words, inserting *uh* [ə] between [i] and [l]. For example, *meal* is [mil], not *mee—uhl* [miəl].

meat — meal   squeak — squeal

eat — eel   deem — deal

seize — seal   neat — kneel

wheat — wheel   heat — heel

Many of the IPA symbols for consonants and the letters of the English alphabet are exactly the same. For instance, the IPA symbol **b** *and the orthographic letter* **b** *both represent the same sound. This will be true of all the consonants which are used in vowel exercises.*

IPA for Singers

B. Transcribe these words into IPA symbols.

*As you read the IPA spelling of these words aloud, be sure to use the correct name of the symbol. [i] is pronounced **ee**, not like the pronoun **I**.*

Speak each word aloud and then transcribe the sounds of the word into IPA symbols. Be sure that you transcribe the symbol for the sound that you hear, and not the orthographic English letter that you are accustomed to seeing written. Each of these words uses the [i] vowel.

1. me [m i]   12. neat _____

2. mean [m i n]   13. knee _____

3. keys [k i z]   14. meat _____

4. piece _____   15. we _____

5. peace _____   16. seed _____

6. peas _____   17. leap _____

7. he _____   18. eve _____

8. feed _____   19. be _____

9. beast _____   20. peep _____

10. fleas _____   21. lea _____

11. fleece _____ 22. please _____

*Listen carefully to all the sounds of the words as you pronounce them aloud. Notice that **piece** and **peace** are both pronounced [pis], and **peas** is [piz]. **Knee** has a silent **k** and is transcribed [ni].*

C. Transcribe these IPA symbols into English words.

1. [it] *eat*   6. [sin] _____

2. [did] _____   7. [mil] _____

3. [kin] _____   8. [tim] _____

4. [hid] _____   9. [fri] _____

5. [tik] _____   10. [krim] _____

22

D. Transcribe these IPA symbols into orthographic spellings.

These are nonsense words and you will have to be creative in your spelling. For instance, [ˌpi ˈzit] might be spelled as *peezeet*.

1. [dik] _____ 5. [ˈi ˌki] _____

2. [ˌi ˈmi] _____ 6. [ˈti ˌki ˌpi] _____

3. [ˈzi ˌli] _____ 7. [ˈni ˌpi] _____

4. [fim] _____ 8. [ˌli ˈbi ˌmi] _____

Remember that accent marks for a primary stressed syllable are above and before the stressed syllable. Refer to page 10 Chapter 2.

E. Vocalize using [i].

Give close attention to maintaining the integrity of the vowel as you sing.

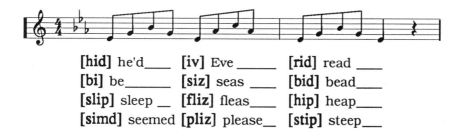

[hid] he'd___ [iv] Eve _____ [rid] read ___
[bi] be_____ [siz] seas ___ [bid] bead___
[slip] sleep _ [fliz] fleas___ [hip] heap___
[simd] seemed [pliz] please_ [stip] steep___

[pik] peek_ [pi] pea _____ [sin] scene_ [si] see
[kin] keen_ [ki] key _____ [nit] neat ___ [ni] knee
[fit] feet___ [fi] fee _____ [wik] weak _ [wi] we

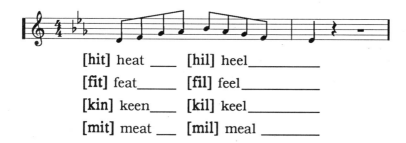

[hit] heat ____ [hil] heel_____
[fit] feat_____ [fil] feel_____
[kin] keen____ [kil] keel_____
[mit] meat ___ [mil] meal _____

Exercises

The forward vowel [ɪ] as in b<u>i</u>t

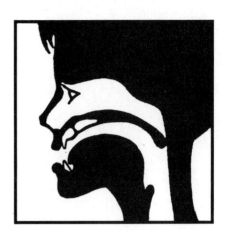

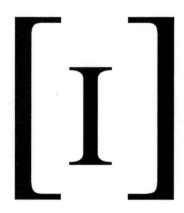

Description

Tongue

The high point of the tongue is forward in the mouth, close to the teeth ridge, slightly lower than *ee* [i]. The tip of the tongue touches the back of the bottom teeth. The sides of the tongue laterally touch the insides of the upper molars.

Jaw

Slightly lower for *ih* [ɪ] than *ee* [i].

Lips

Unrounded, more open than *ee* [i].

Soft Palate

Raised, closing off the nasal passageway.

Common Problems

Some people tend to nasalize the *ih* [ɪ] vowel when it precedes *m*, *n*, and *ng*.

A. Practice the ih [ɪ] sound.

Read these sounds aloud.

[bɪ] (*as in bit*), [bɪ], [bɪ], [bɪ], [bɪ]

[pɪ] (*as in pick*), [pɪ], [pɪ], [pɪ], [pɪ]

[ɪb], [ɪp], [ɪb], [ɪp]

Read aloud to contrast the *ee* [i] and *ih* [ɪ] sounds.

[bi bɪ]	[pi pɪ]	[bi bɪ]
[ɪb ib]	[ɪp ip]	[ɪb ib]

Read aloud these English words using [i] and [ɪ].

[bid] — [bɪd]	[bit] — [bɪt]
[fit] — [fɪt]	[biz] — ['bɪ ˌzɪ]
[il] — [ɪl]	[it] — [ɪt]

Read aloud these nonsense words.

[ig] — [ɪg]	[zi] — [zɪ]
['i ˌmi] — ['ɪ ˌmɪ]	[di] — [dɪ]

Read aloud each following pair of words. Avoid nasality in the second column where the [ɪ] vowel precedes the nasal consonants *m*, *n*, and *ng*.

[ɪ] preceding non-nasal consonants		[ɪ] preceding nasal consonants
mitten	—	Minnie
differ	—	dinner
rids	—	rinse
tip	—	tin
lift	—	lint
mitt	—	mint
wit	—	winter
pit	—	pinto

B. Transcribe these words into IPA symbols.

Speak each word aloud and then transcribe the sounds of the word into IPA symbols. Be sure that you transcribe the symbol for the sound you hear, and not the orthographic letter that you are accustomed to seeing written. Each of these words uses the [ɪ] sound.

1. him ___[hɪm]___   6. his _____

*The word **women**, although it doesn't appear to have an [ɪ] sound, actually has two! ['wɪ mɪn].*

2. women _____   7. kill _____

3. fin _____   8. fizz _____

4. mill _____   9. din _____

*The letter **s** is often pronounced **z** as in **kids** [kɪdz].*

5. kids _____   10. gigged _____

*When transcribing the word **Billy** ['bɪ lɪ], be sure that you do not use the capital letter **B**. A capital letter does not have a different sound from a lower case letter. The sound of both **b** and **B** is [b].*

The following words use [i] and [ɪ]. Transcribe into IPA symbols.

1. fleet _____   8. mid _____

2. give _____   9. Billy _____

*How do you pronounce the **y** at the end of words like **Billy, lily,** or **hilly?** Some people say [i] while others say [ɪ]. Notice that this text uses [ɪ] for the final, unstressed **y**.*

3. speak _____   10. lily _____

4. milk _____   11. receive _____

5. meek _____   12. believe _____

*Another unstressed [ɪ] occurs on the first syllable of **believe** and **receive**. Unstressing in our language will be discussed in Chapter 6.*

6. tint _____   13. hilly _____

7. sit _____   14. tease _____

C. Transcribe the IPA symbols into English words. This exercise uses both [i] and [ɪ].

1. [hit] _____   5. [liv] _____

2. [hɪt] _____   6. [lɪv] _____

3. [dip] _____   7. [sip] _____

4. [dɪp] _____   8. [sɪp] _____

D. Transcribe the IPA symbols of these nonsense words into orthographic spellings.

1. ['wi ˌzɪ] _____   4. [hɪg]_____

2. [fɪp] _____   5. [zɪb] _____

3. ['i ˌkɪ] _____   6. [kɪr] _____

If you have difficulty finding the stress of a word, refer to page 10 for assistance.

E. Vocalize using [i] and [ɪ]. Give close attention to maintaining the integrity of these vowels as you sing.

Be aware of the vowel in each word. Know if it is [i] or [ɪ]

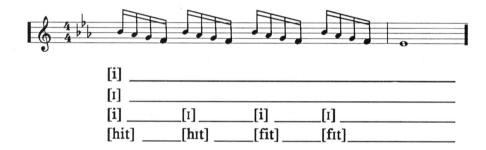

[i] _____
[ɪ] _____
[i] _____[ɪ] _____[i] _____[ɪ] _____
[hit] _____[hɪt] _____[fit] _____[fɪt]_____

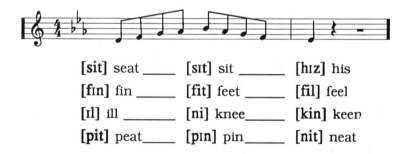

[sit] seat _____ [sɪt] sit _____ [hɪz] his

[fɪn] fin _____ [fit] feet _____ [fil] feel

[ɪl] ill _____ [ni] knee_____ [kin] keen

[pit] peat_____ [pɪn] pin_____ [nit] neat

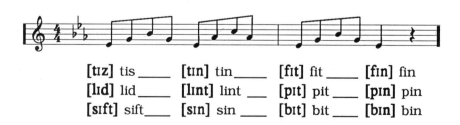

[tɪz] tis _____ [tɪn] tin_____ [fɪt] fit _____ [fɪn] fin

[lɪd] lid_____ [lɪnt] lint ___ [pɪt] pit ___ [pɪn] pin

[sɪft] sift_____ [sɪn] sin ___ [bɪt] bit ___ [bɪn] bin

Exercises

The pure vowel [e] as in *ch<u>a</u>otic*
The diphthong [eɪ] as in *b<u>ai</u>t*

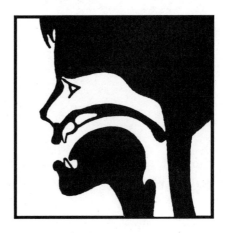

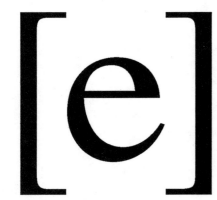

Description

The mid, forward vowel **[e]**, as in *chaotic*, is rarely used in its pure form in American English, although it is occasionally found in unstressed syllables.

In American English, the diphthong **[eɪ]** is consistently used in place of the pure **[e]** and may be considered an allophone of **[e]**.

Tongue

For pure **[e]**, the tip of the tongue touches the back of the bottom teeth. The front of the tongue is raised and brought forward in the mouth, elevated to a point close to the roof of the mouth but lower than **[ɪ]**. The sides of the tongue laterally touch the upper side molars.

The diphthong **[eɪ]** is created when the pure **[e]** is released with a quick upward movement of the tongue to **[ɪ]**, thus creating the diphthong.

Jaw

Slightly lower for **[e]** than for **[ɪ]**.

Lips

Unrounded.

Soft Palate

Raised, closing off the nasal passageway.

Common Problems

The substitution of diphthongal [eɪ] for pure [e] in foreign languages. In foreign languages, diphthongal [eɪ] must be avoided.

The lowering of the tongue to an *eh* [ɛ] position, as in *bet*, which creates a triphthong, a vowel with three parts. *Wait* [weɪt] becomes [wɛeɪt].

The insertion of *uh* [ə] between [eɪ] and [l], as when the word *sail* sounds like *say-uhl* [seɪ əl].

It may surprise many beginning singers that long *ā* as in *came* is pronounced as a diphthong by nearly every speaker of American English and that the pure [e] as in *chaotic* is rarely used in English. To bring the diphthong [eɪ] into your awareness, speak the word *aim* aloud in slow motion while noticing what your tongue does. Just before the *m* of *aim*, you should be able to feel the front part of your tongue move forward and up from [e] to [ɪ]. Listen to the vowel change. This gliding tongue movement produces the diphthong.

Any time there is a movement of the tongue, lips, or jaw when producing a vowel, a diphthong occurs.

Diphthong is pronounced **dif-thong** [ˈdɪf θɔŋ]

Native speakers of English so consistently use diphthongal [eɪ] instead of pure [e] that many have difficulty distinguishing the difference between the two sounds. They hear diphthongal [eɪ] as an indivisible unit which they identify as the pure vowel [e]. Read aloud the following words slowly. Feel the gliding movement of the tongue as it moves from [e] to [ɪ] to produce the diphthong [eɪ].

aim, came, bay, may, hay, made, Kate, blame, flame.

To isolate the pure [e] sound, try speaking the word *hay* aloud in slow motion without moving the tongue to [ɪ]. The word will sound incomplete, strange, and unfamiliar to most Americans. If you do not make a gliding movement with the tongue, you will be producing a pure [e].

Because most Americans use diphthongal [eɪ] in place of pure [e], many phoneticians consider diphthongal [eɪ] as an *allophone* of the phoneme [e]. The major reference book on American pronunciation, A Pronouncing Dictionary of American English, by Kenyon and Knott, and many other phonetic texts, choose to use the phoneme [e] to represent the allophone [eɪ].

	This Text	Kenyon and Knott
tame	[teɪm]	[tem]
cake	[keɪk]	[kek]
aim	[eɪm]	[em]
bait	[beɪt]	[bet]

There are two reasons why this manual uses the symbol [eɪ] instead of [e] in transcriptions. First, the skillful pronunciation of diphthongal [eɪ] is critical to stylistic singing in English. In sustained melodies, words are prolonged and the diphthong is slowed down. Singers must make a choice about how to sing it. How long should [e] be sustained? At what point does the tongue glide to [ɪ]? Should the glide be quick or slow?

In bel canto or classical music, the pure [e] is sustained as long as possible and the short quick glide to the second vowel [ɪ] is put off until the very end. Popular music often approaches the diphthong differently, slowing down the gliding movement, giving more duration to the second vowel [ɪ], sometimes even changing it to the more close *ee* [i]. See the following example:

Classical singing:	sing *aim*	[e -----------------------------ɪm]
Popular singing:	sing *aim*	[e -------------- ɪ ----------m]
	or sing *aim*	[eɪ -------------------------m]
	or sing *aim*	[ei -------------------------m]

Secondly, while the English language uses diphthongal [eɪ], Italian, French, German and other languages use only the pure [e]. Singers who cannot isolate the pure [e] and unknowingly use the diphthongal [eɪ] mar their singing of these languages with a heavy American accent. Conversely, foreigners who wish to speak or sing English without an accent must learn to use the diphthongal [eɪ].

A large part of singing artistry is to have sufficient control and flexibility to be able to make these articulation differences in diction.

A. Practice the diphthong [eɪ].

Read aloud these sounds.

[beɪ] [peɪ] [beɪ] [peɪ]
[eɪb] [eɪp] [eɪb] [eɪp]

Read aloud these paired words. In the second column of words, avoid inserting *uh* [ə] between [eɪ] and [l].

say	sail
way	wail
ate	ale
mate	male
flake	flail
skate	scale
paid	pale

Read aloud these English words using [eɪ]

[teɪk] [meɪk] [deɪn] [eɪk]

Read aloud these nonsense words using [eɪ]

[zeɪg] ['eɪ ˌvɪt] [heɪk] [weɪm]

B. Practice the pure [e].

Read aloud these English words using pure [e] in unstressed syllables.

ch<u>a</u>otic	[ke 'ɑ tɪk]
v<u>a</u>cation	[ve 'keɪ ʃən]
Mond<u>ay</u>	['mʌn de]
n<u>a</u>tivity	[ne 'tɪ və tɪ]
f<u>a</u>tality	[fe 'tæ lə tɪ]

Read aloud these sounds using pure [e], not diphthongal [eɪ]. Do not permit your tongue to glide to [ɪ].

[pe] [pe] [be] [be]
[te] [te] [me] [me]
[e]   [e]   [e]   [e]

Read aloud these sounds to contrast pure [e] and diphthongal [eɪ].

[be beɪ] [be beɪ] [be beɪ]
[beɪ be be beɪ] [peɪ pe pe peɪ]

Read aloud these nonsense words using pure [e].

['e ˌme]   [tes]   [ˌle 'ne]   [ˌe 'ti]

Read aloud these Italian words using pure [e].

venti	['ven ti]	(twenty)
chè	[ke]	(for, because)
e	[e]	(and)
tre	[tre]	(three)

Read aloud these German words using pure [e].

The symbol [ː] indicates that a vowel sound is sustained for a longer duration than one without the symbol [ː]. For example, [eː] is sustained longer than [e].

See	[zeː]	(lake)
lebt	[leːpt]	(from verb leben, *to live*)
er	[eːr]	(he)
Beet	[beːt]	(bed)

Read aloud these French words using pure [e].

French speakers and singers articulate the [e] vowel with the high point of the tongue nearer the teeth ridge than in English. To Americans, the [e] sounds almost like [i]. This is an example of an allophone of [e].

élite	[e lit]	(elite)
et	[e]	(and)
été	[e te]	(summer)
vider	[vi de]	(to empty)

**C. Transcribe these words into IPA symbols.
All the words use [eɪ].**

1. bales [beɪlz]   9. bay _____
2. dale _____   10. may _____
3. wait _____   11. Fay _____
4. weight _____   12. feign _____
5. ate _____   13. great _____
6. deign _____   14. grate _____
7. vail _____   15. grail _____
8. fail _____   16. hail _____

D. Transcribe these IPA symbols into English words. Each word uses the [eɪ] sound.

1. [keɪp] _____   6. [peɪ] _____
2. [meɪl] _____   7. [eɪs] _____
3. [geɪ] _____   8. [veɪs] _____
4. [veɪn] _____   9. [seɪm] _____
5. [neɪp] _____   10. [steɪt] _____

E. Transcribe these words into IPA symbols.
The words include [i ɪ eɪ].

1. seal _____   7. lid _____
2. reek _____   8. came _____
3. hay _____   9. kiss _____
4. Kate _____   10. see _____
5. teak _____   11. veal _____
6. tick _____   12. tail _____

F. Transcribe these IPA symbols into English words. The words contain [i ɪ eɪ].

1. [lik] _____   9. [dim] _____
2. [lɪk] _____   10. [dɪm] _____
3. [leɪk] _____   11. [deɪt] _____
4. [mit] _____   12. [min] _____
5. [mɪt] _____   13. [meɪn] _____
6. [meɪt] _____   14. [stid] _____
7. [pɪt] _____   15. [stɪk] _____
8. [peɪd] _____   16. [steɪk] _____

G. Transcribe the IPA symbols of these nonsense words into orthographic letters.

1. ['ɪk ˌneɪ] _____
2. ['meɪ ˌdi] _____
3. [ˌfɪ 'keɪ] _____
4. ['vɪt ˌfi] _____
5. ['heɪ ˌni] _____

6. [ˌpɪ 'lid] _____
7. ['ɡreɪk] _____
8. ['eɪ ˌsɪp] _____
9. ['zɪt ˌmeɪ] _____
10. ['teɪ ˌki] _____

H. Vocalize on the forward vowels [i], [ɪ], and diphthongal [eɪ].

Give close attention to maintaining the integrity of these vowels as you sing.
Sing these words which contain a diphthongal [eɪ].
Notice the movement of your tongue. Sustain the first part of the diphthong [e] and then, *only as you release the tone,* glide to the second vowel [ɪ].

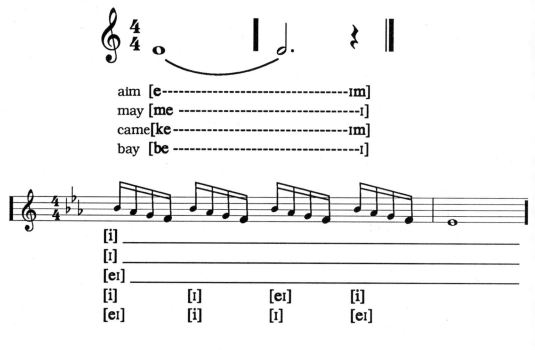

aim [e--------------------------------ɪm]
may [me --------------------------------ɪ]
came[ke--------------------------------ɪm]
bay [be --------------------------------ɪ]

[i] _____
[ɪ] _____
[eɪ] _____

[i]	[ɪ]	[eɪ]	[i]
[eɪ]	[i]	[ɪ]	[eɪ]

[lik] leek   [lɪk] lick   [leɪk] lake
[rid] read   [rɪd] rid   [reɪd] raid
[mit] meet   [mɪt] mitt   [meɪt] mate

I. Vocalize, clearly articulating the pure [e] sounds.

Give close attention to maintaining the integrity of the vowel sounds as you sing. *Do not use diphthongal* [eɪ].

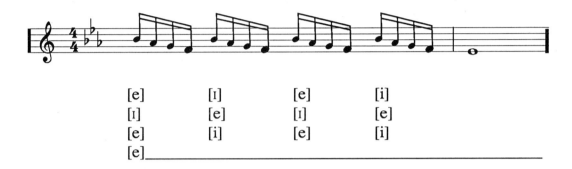

[e]	[ɪ]	[e]	[i]
[ɪ]	[e]	[ɪ]	[e]
[e]	[i]	[e]	[i]
[e]_____			

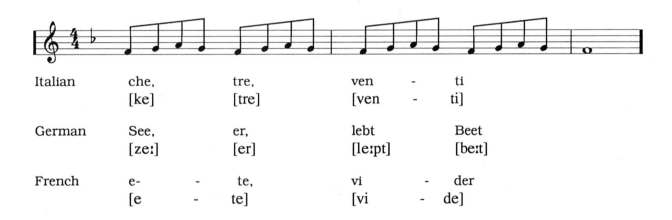

Italian	che,	tre,	ven	-	ti
	[ke]	[tre]	[ven	-	ti]
German	See,	er,	lebt		Beet
	[zeː]	[er]	[leːpt]		[beːt]
French	e-	-	te,	vi	-	der
	[e	-	te]	[vi	-	de]

Exercises

The forward vowel [ε] as in b<u>e</u>t

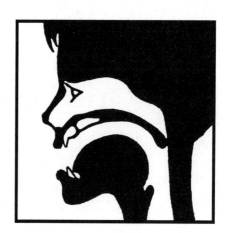

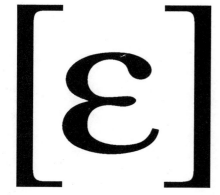

Description

Tongue

For [ε] the front of the tongue is arched, brought forward in the mouth, and elevated to a point midway to the roof of the mouth, lower than [eɪ]. The tip touches the back of the bottom teeth. The sides of the tongue touch the inside of the upper teeth.

Jaw

Slightly lower for [ε] than for [eɪ].

Lips

Unrounded and more open for [ε] than for [e].

Soft Palate

Raised, closing off the nasal passageway.

Common Problems

The substitution of [ɪ] for [ε] as in *git* for *get*.
The substitution of [eɪ] for [ε] as in *haid* for *head*.
The substitution of ă [æ] for [ε] as in *gas* for *guess*.
The substitution of *ûr* [ɜ] for [ε] as in *Amuhrica* for *America*.
The insertion of *uh* [ə] between [ε] and [l] as in *well* (*weh-uhl*).

A. Practice the [ɛ] sound as in bet.

Read aloud these sounds.

[bɛ] [pɛ] [bɛ] [pɛ]
[ɛp] [ɛb] [ɛp] [ɛb]

Read aloud these words to clarify the [ɛ] sound.

red

bed

desk

step

pest

left

death

check

Read aloud these word pairs to contrast [ɪ] and [ɛ].

[ɪ]	[ɛ]
bill	bell
pit	pet
hid	head
pin	pen
tin	ten
tint	tent
lint	lent
rinse	rents
twin	twenty

The substitution of [ɪ] for [ɛ] is a common distortion which tends to occur before *t*, *m* and *n*, such as *git* for *get*, *timpt* for *tempt*, or *pin* for *pen*.

Read aloud these paired words. Maintain [ɛ] in both lists. Do not use the [ɪ] sound in words in the second list.

head	hem
Ted	ten, tenth
med	men, meant
bed	Ben
dead	den, dent
ebb	ember

Read aloud these paired words to contrast the [eɪ] and [ɛ] sounds.

[eɪ]	[ɛ]
bait	bet
mate	met
sail	sell
tail	tell
taste	test
gate	get
mace	mess

Pronouncing [eɪ] is another common distortion of the vowel sound [ɛ], though in some words, it is considered an acceptable variation. Avoid saying *haid* for *head* or *laig* for *leg*. Be sure to use [ɛ] in such words as *egg*, *bed*, *measure*, and *pleasure*.

Read aloud these paired words. Maintain [ɛ] in both lists. Do not use [eɪ] in the second list.

ledge	leg
Ed	egg
pet	Peggy
tread	treasure
pled	pleasure

Saying [æ] as in *bad* in place of [ɛ] is a third distortion that is occasionally heard. The word *yes*, for example, may sound something like *yass*, or *guess* like *gas*.

Read aloud these words to contrast [ɛ] and [æ] sounds.

[ɛ]	[æ]
yes	yass
guess	gas

Still another distortion is using *ûr* [ɝ] as in *burr* in place of [ɛ], as in pronouncing *America* as *Amuh-rica*.

Read aloud these words. Use [ɛ], not the *ûr* [ɝ] sound (as in *burr*).

very

American

where

library

Read aloud these nonsense words using [i ɪ eɪ ɛ].

[hig]　[hɪg]　[heɪg]　[hɛg]

['i ˌti]　['ɪ ˌtɪ]　['eɪ ˌteɪ]　['ɛ ˌtɛ]

['li ˌvi]　['lɪ ˌvɪ]　['leɪ ˌveɪ]　['lɛ ˌvɛ]

[spiz]　[spɪz]　[speɪz]　[spɛz]

B. Transcribe these words into IPA symbols. All words use [ɛ].

1. cent　[sɛnt]　　8. any _____
2. best _____　9. guessed_____
3. kelp _____　10. tempts _____
4. dents _____　11. blend _____
5. vet _____　12. bell _____
6. petty _____　13. met _____
7. penny _____　14. many _____

C. Transcribe these IPA symbols into English words.
Each word uses [ɛ].

1. [sɛd] _____   6. [ɛnd] _____
2. [fɛl] _____   7. [blɛd] _____
3. [hɛlp] _____   8. [mɛnt] _____
4. [ɛlf] _____   9. [lɛft] _____
5. [wɛd] _____   10. [bɛs] _____

Remember—capital letters are not used in IPA transcriptions. [bɛs] = Bess.

D. Transcribe these English words into IPA symbols. This exercise includes [i ɪ eɪ ɛ].

1. mailed _____   11. felled _____
2. aimed _____   12. played _____
3. ebb _____   13. still _____
4. peak _____   14. sled _____
5. knell _____   15. knit _____
6. win _____   16. belt _____
7. wend _____   17. fade _____
8. way _____   18. fed _____
9. debt _____   19. fit _____
10. date _____   20. feet _____

E. Transcribe these IPA symbols into English words. These words use [i ɪ eɪ ɛ].

1. [geɪp] _____   6. [deɪ] _____
2. [mɪl] _____   7. [dɛk] _____
3. [gis] _____   8. [fɪst] _____
4. [veɪl] _____   9. [geɪm] _____
5. [lɛt] _____   10. [stɛp] _____

F. Transcribe the IPA symbols of these nonsense words into orthographic spellings.

1. [ˌgɛ ˈri] _____   4. [ˈkeɪ ˌkɛ] _____

2. [ˈweɪ ˌbɛ] _____   5. [fis] _____

3. [ˌlɛ ˈleɪ] _____   6. [ˌɛ ˈpɛt] _____

G. Vocalize using [i ɪ eɪ ɛ].

Pay close attention to maintaining the integrity of these vowels as you sing.

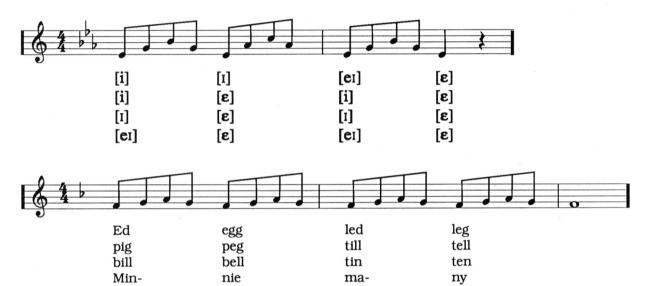

[i]	[ɪ]	[eɪ]	[ɛ]
[i]	[ɛ]	[i]	[ɛ]
[ɪ]	[ɛ]	[ɪ]	[ɛ]
[eɪ]	[ɛ]	[eɪ]	[ɛ]

Ed	egg	led	leg
pig	peg	till	tell
bill	bell	tin	ten
Min-	nie	ma-	ny

Exercises

The forward vowel [æ] as in b<u>a</u>t

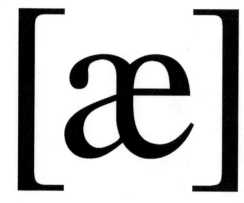

Description

Tongue

The high point of the tongue is forward in the mouth, slightly lower than for [ɛ]. The tip of the tongue touches the back of the bottom teeth. The sides of the tongue may or may not touch the upper back teeth depending upon the speaker's personal articulation habit, but for fuller resonance in singing, the sides of the tongue do not touch the upper back teeth.

Because the space between the tongue and the roof of the mouth is open, and the high point of the tongue is forward, this vowel is called an open, forward vowel.

Jaw

Slightly lower for [æ] than for [ɛ].

Lips

Unrounded and more open than for [ɛ].

Soft Palate

Raised, closing off the nasal passageway.

Common Problems

The insertion of *uh* [ə] after [æ] before a final consonant, as in *ha-uht* for *hat.*

Nasalizing [æ] when it precedes *m, n,* or *ng.*

A. Practice the [æ] sound as in *bat*.

Read aloud these sounds and words.

[bæ]	[pæ]	[bæ]	[pæ]
[æp]	[æb]	[æp]	[æb]
[mæd]	[hæd]	[blæst]	[dæd]

Read aloud these words to contrast [ɛ] and [æ].

[ɛ]	[æ]
Ed	add
pest	past
men	man
bed	bad
said	sad
then	than

Read aloud these words to contrast [eɪ] and [æ].

[eɪ]	[æ]
aid	add
cane	can
plain	plan
lame	lamb
pain	pan

Read aloud, being careful not to nasalize the vowel in the second column. Both columns use [æ].

sad	Sam
cad	can
mad	man
dab	damp
sag	sang
hat	hang

Read aloud these words, being careful not to insert *uh* [ə] between [æ] and the final consonant. *Man* is not *ma-uhn* [mæən].

add	man	can
hat	fan	bad
Hal	stamp	trap
plaid	cat	hand

Read aloud these nonsense words using [i ɪ eɪ ɛ æ].

[æv]   [ɪkt]   [bæp]   [zæm]   [neɪt]

['i ˌdi]   ['ɪ ˌdɪ]   ['eɪ ˌɡeɪ]   ['ɛ ˌɡe]   ['æ ˌɡæ]

[ˌɛ 'mæ]   ['tæ ˌneɪ]   ['kɛ ˌmɪ]   [mæz]   [fɪk]

B. Transcribe into IPA symbols. All the words contain [æ].

*The orthographic letter **x** has the sound of [ks].*

*In the word **lamb,** the **b** is silent.*

*An apostrophe is not written in IPA: **can't** is [kænt].*

1. back	[bæk]	9. lass	[læs]
2. cat	[kæt]	10. adds	[ædz]
3. dab	[dæb]	11. have	[hæv]
4. bad	[bæd]	12. ham	[hæm]
5. axe	[æks]	13. lamb	[læm]
6. pad	[pæd]	14. can't	[kænt]
7. ant	[ænt]	15. hack	[hæk]
8. rat	[ræt]	16. black	[blæk]

C. Transcribe these IPA symbols into English words. Each of these words contains the [æ] sound.

1. [ækt]	act	5. [tænz]	
2. [hæm]	ham	6. [pæk]	pack
3. [ræt]	rat	7. [tæk]	tack
4. [bræn]	bran	8. [stæmp]	stamp

D. Transcribe these words into IPA symbols. These words include [i ɪ eɪ ɛ æ].

1. lack		11. gas	
2. leek		12. lick	
3. say		13. let	
4. get		14. tab	
5. hat		15. gave	
6. pet		16. class	
7. fat		17. seat	
8. mane		18. mere	
9. Phoenix		19. rack	
10. lily		20. wreck	

E. Transcribe these IPA symbols into English words.

1. ['tɛk sɪs] _Texas_   6. [sænd] _sand_
2. ['tæk sɪz] _taxes_   7. [blɛst] _blessed_
3. [pɛst] _pest_   8. [blænd] _bland_
4. [pæst] _past_   9. [ski] _ski_
5. [leɪk] _lake_   10. [lɪv] _live_

F. Transcribe the IPA symbols of these nonsense words into orthographic letters.

1. ['æ ˌzɪk] _azik_   4. [ˌfɪ 'pi] _fipee_
2. [neɪf] _nayf_   5. ['bæ ˌbɪ] _babih_
3. ['fæ ˌteɪ] _fatay_   6. ['ɪ ˌzɪ] _izih_

**E. Vocalize, using the forward vowels [i ɪ eɪ ɛ æ].
Maintain the integrity of each vowel as you sing.**

[i]   [ɪ]   [eɪ]   [ɛ]   [æ]

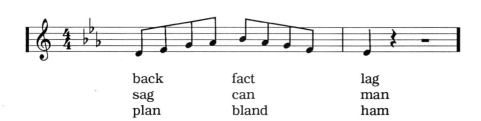

back   fact   lag
sag   can   man
plan   bland   ham

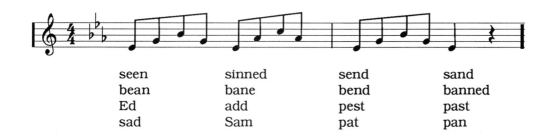

seen   sinned   send   sand
bean   bane   bend   banned
Ed   add   pest   past
sad   Sam   pat   pan

45

Exercises

The forward vowel [a], found in English diphthongs [aɪ] and [aʊ] as in the words *by* and *house*.

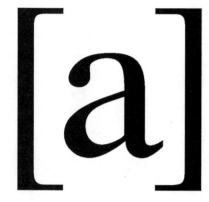

Description

Tongue

The high point of the tongue lies lower in the mouth for *bright ah* **[a]** than for **[æ]** as in *bat*, but higher than for the back *dark ah* **[ɑ]** as in *father*. The tongue tip rests behind the back of the bottom teeth. The space between the tongue and the roof of the mouth is the most open of the forward vowels.

Jaw

Low position.

Lips

Open and unrounded.

Soft Palate

Raised, closing off the nasal passageway.

Common Problems

The substitution of **[æ]** for forward, *bright ah* **[a]**.

The substitution of back *dark ah* **[ɑ]** for forward *bright ah* **[a]**.

Many Americans have difficulty identifying and isolating the *bright ah* [a] because, in General American English, it is almost always part of a diphthong and seldom used in isolation. In foreign languages, however, *bright ah* [a] is frequently used. Singers who perform songs in foreign languages must be able to identify and produce this vowel sound.

One rather dependable way for Americans to isolate the *bright ah* [a] is to prolong the diphthongal sound [aɪ] as in *by, high, might,* and *hi.* Speak aloud the word *Hi!*, drawling it out in slow motion speech. It will sound like: *hah.....ih.* Feel the movement of the tongue as it changes from *ah* [a] to *ih* [ɪ]. Listen to the first part of the diphthong and you will hear the *bright ah* [a].

The *bright ah* [a] sound exists in two English diphthongs: [aɪ] as in *Hi!* and [aʊ] as in *house.* A second example can help you identify [a]. Say the word *house* in slow motion. Start with *ha* and slowly move your lips to *oo* as in *ooze.* Again you can hear the *bright ah* [a] as the first part of the diphthong.

In addition to finding the forward *bright ah* [a] in English diphthongs [aɪ] and [aʊ], it can also be found in the dialects of those in New England who say *pahk the cahr* for *park the car* or pronounce *Boston* as [ˈba stən].

Americans tend to substitute two other vowel sounds for [a]. The first substitution is using [æ], as in *bat,* instead of *bright ah* [a]. It occurs when the speaker brings the tongue too far up and forward in the mouth. The second substitution is *dark ah* [ɑ], as in *father,* which occurs when the speaker brings the tongue too far back and down. The back, *dark ah* [ɑ] will be fully discussed in the next chapter.

These sounds are very similar. Only the slightest movements of the tongue create the difference among these three sounds. The following exercises will help you isolate the forward *bright ah* [a] sound and differentiate it from the lower *dark ah* [ɑ] and the higher, forward vowel [æ].

A. Practice the *bright ah* [a] sound.

Read aloud these sounds.

[ba]	[pa]	[ba]	[pa]
[ap]	[ab]	[ap]	[ab]

Read these words with a Southern drawl and identify the sound of **[a]**. Each *bright ah* **[a]** will be underlined.

H<u>ah</u> ya doin'? (How are you doing?)

Wh<u>ah</u>, <u>ah</u>'m f<u>ah</u>n! (Why, I'm fine!)

<u>Ah</u>'m goin'. (I'm going.)

Read these phrases with a New England dialect. Each *bright ah* **[a]** is underlined.

P<u>ah</u>k the c<u>ah</u>r (Park the car)

In the b<u>ah</u>n (In the barn)

In the g<u>ah</u>den (In the garden)

Read aloud these sounds to contrast **[æ]** and forward *bright ah* **[a]**. Drop your jaw to a low position. Feel the forward and upward movement of the tongue as you go from **[a]** to **[æ]**.

[a] — [æ]　　**[a] — [æ]**　　**[a] — [æ]**　　**[a] — [æ]**

Read aloud these sounds to practice **[æ]**, the forward *bright ah* **[a]** and the back *dark ah* **[ɑ]**. Drop your jaw to a low position for all three vowels. Feel the movement of your tongue as you go from one vowel to another. The tongue is in its highest position for **[æ]**. It moves slightly down for **[a]** and again slightly down for **[ɑ]**.

[æ]	[a]	[ɑ]
[æ]	[a]	[ɑ]
[æ]	[a]	[ɑ]

[æ]	[a]	[æ]
[a]	[ɑ]	[a]

B. Pronounce these French words using bright ah [a].

1. glace	[glas]	(translates as ice-cream)
2. tard	[tar]	(late)
3. passer	[pa se]	(to pass)
4. par	[par]	(by, through)

C. Pronounce these German words using bright ah [a].

1. Tat	[tat]	(deed)
2. das	[das]	(that)
3. Hast	[hast]	(hurry)
4. ganz	[gants]	(all)

D. Pronounce these Italian words using bright ah [a].

1. caraffa	[ka'rafːfa]	(*decanter*)
2. bacca	[bakːka]	(*berry*)
3. bimba	[bim ba]	(*little girl*)
4. landa	['lan da]	(*moor*)

*Be careful to use **bright ah** [a] for the final syllables of these Italian words. Do not use **uh** [ə].*

Chapter 4 Worksheet

Transcribe these words into IPA symbols.
These words contain all the forward vowels.

1. betray [bɪ ˈtreɪ]
2. casket [ˈkæ skɪt]
3. believe [bɪ ˈliv]
4. creek [krik]
5. grand [grænd]

6. impale [ɪm ˈpeɪl]
7. case [keɪs]
8. gave [geɪv]
9. hat [hæt]
10. fleeced [flist]

11. headed [ˈhɛ dɪd]
12. flabby [ˈflæ bi]
13. heat [hit]
14. crack [kræk]
15. impel [ɪm ˈpɛl]

16. steam [stim]
17. tape [teɪp]
18. impressive [ɪm ˈprɛ sɪv]
19. palate [ˈpæ lɪt]
20. taxi [ˈtæ ksi]

21. cranberry [ˈkræn bɛri]
22. flat [flæt]
23. fled [flɛd]
24. blaze [bleɪz]
25. flack [flæk]

26. still [stɪl]
27. grade [greɪd]
28. pansy [ˈpæ nzi]
29. black [blæk]
30. galley [ˈgæ li]

31. gasp [gæsp]
32. kelp [kɛlp]
33. pegged [pɛgd]
34. knack [næk]
35. key [ki]

36. pin [pɪn]
37. waft [waft]
38. rip [rɪp]
39. kneaded [ˈni dɪd]
40. maize [meɪz]

Chapter 4 Worksheet

Transcribe these IPA symbols into English words.

1. ['seɪ krɪd]   sacred
2. ['mæ lɪs]   malice
3. ['peɪl ˌfeɪs]   paleface
4. ['ri ˌleɪ]   relay
5. ['pɛn ˌsɪv]   pensive

6. [rɪ 'læps]   relapse
7. [prɪnt]   print
8. [rɪ 'zɪst]   resist
9. ['sɛn trɪ]
10. [pækt]   pact

11. [ˌpri 'sid]   pre seed
12. ['mæ lɪt]   mallet
13. ['pri fɪks]   prefix
14. [ræft]   raft
15. [spreɪ]   spray

16. [snæk]   snack
17. ['reɪn dɪr]   reindeer
18. [spɛr]   spare
19. [skeɪt]   skate
20. [lɪv]   live

CHAPTER 5
BACK VOWELS

Introduction to Back Vowels

Those vowels which are articulated with the high point of the tongue in the back of the mouth are called the *back vowels*. Each back vowel is produced with the tip of the tongue touching the back of the bottom front teeth and a raised soft palate, closing off the nasal passage. Four of the five back vowels are produced with rounded lips. The back vowels of English are:

ōō **[u]** as in b<u>oo</u>t.

ŏŏ **[ʊ]** as in b<u>oo</u>k.

oh **[oʊ]** as in b<u>oa</u>t.

aw **[ɔ]** as in b<u>ou</u>ght.

ah **[ɑ]** as in b<u>o</u>x, or *f<u>a</u>ther.*

Pronunciations of Words

The standards for pronunciations are determined by the pronunciations of leading American speakers: national news commentators, actors, educators, civic leaders and social leaders. This speech is referred to as General American dialect.

In addition to General American dialect, there are regional dialects. Large geographical regions have their own standard pronunciations derived from the educated public in that region. The result is a lack of national consistency in the pronunciations of words, especially words with back vowels. For example, the first vowel in the words *horrid, water* or *office* may be pronounced either *aw* [ɔ] or *ah* [ɑ] depending upon the geographical background of the speaker.

horrid	['hɔ rɪd]	or	['hɑ rɪd]
water	['wɔ tɚ]	or	['wɑ tɚ]
office	['ɔ fɪs]	or	['ɑ fɪs]

A Pronouncing Dictionary of American English by Kenyon and Knott* is an excellent source for pronunciations. This dictionary gives the IPA transcriptions of words as spoken in General American dialect and also lists other standard pronunciations from regional dialects, such as Eastern, Southern, or Southwestern.

If your pronunciations do not agree with the ones suggested in this text, refer to A Pronouncing Dictionary of American English to determine whether you are using a standard or non-standard pronunciation. You can then determine for yourself whether it would be appropriate to change your pronunciations. The General American dialect is a good choice for classical singing.

*A Pronouncing Dictionary of American English, Kenyon and Knott, C.& G. Merriam Co., Publishers, Springfield, Mass. 01101

Practice the sounds of the back vowels.

Read aloud these similar words to contrast the sounds of the back vowels.

Contrast the sounds of the various back vowels. Become familiar with the IPA symbol which represents each sound.

[u]	[ʊ]	[oʊ]	[ɔ]	[ɑ]
boot	book	boat	bought	box
pool	pull	pole	Paul	pot
coo	cook	coat	caught	cot
Sioux	soot	sown	saw	sot
roux	rook	wrote	wrought	rot
loot	look	loan	law	lot

Be especially careful to use sufficient rounding of the lips for [u] [ʊ] [oʊ] and [ɔ]. For [ɑ] the lips are open and unrounded.

Diphthongal [oʊ] is consistently used in American English in place of pure [o] (see Chapter 5 Exercises).

In addition to the five back vowels listed above, there is another sound, referred to as *short o* [ɒ], which can be heard when speakers with a British accent say the words *not, got, lot, lost*. A standard allophone of both *aw* [ɔ] and *ah* [ɑ], the *short o* [ɒ] occurs in Eastern dialect and occasionally in some other regional dialects. As you read the lists of back vowels, try to isolate the pure sounds of *aw* [ɔ] and *ah* [ɑ] indicated by these words. The allophone [ɒ] and its relation to singing will be discussed on page 71.

Whisper the following list of vowels several times.

Whisper ōō [u] (as in *boot*)

Whisper ŏŏ [ʊ] (as in *book*)

Whisper *oh* [oʊ] (as in *boat*)

Whisper *aw* [ɔ] (as in *bought*)

Whisper *ah* [ɑ] (as in *father*)

[u]

As you whisper the list of vowels, notice that several changes will occur in the size and shape of your mouth as you proceed down the list from [u] to [ɑ]. Your jaw lowers progressively and your lips open. Your lips have the greatest rounding for [u]. On [ʊ] the lips relax slightly, but remain rounded. For [o] and [ɔ] the lips again become more rounded. Finally, as you whisper [ɑ], your lips become unrounded and your jaw is in its lowest position.

You might find it helpful to look in a mirror as you whisper these vowels. Notice that the tip of the tongue touches the back of the bottom front teeth for all back vowels while the other changes are taking place. The positions of the tongue, jaw and lips during the production of each of the back vowels are also illustrated in the diagrams on the right.

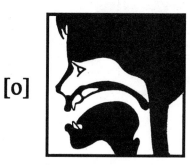

[ʊ]

Transfer the ease and clarity of the whispered vowels into speech.

After whispering *oo* [u] several times, then speak *oo* [u] on a pitch in your normal speaking range. Do not change the vowel sound nor the physical shape of the vowel when transferring from whispering to speaking. Maintain a relaxed jaw and throat. Repeat the same process for each vowel.

[o]

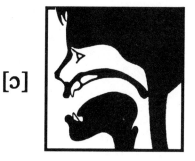

whisper [u u u]   speak [u u u] (as in *boot*)

whisper [ʊ ʊ ʊ]   speak [ʊ ʊ ʊ] (as in *book*)

whisper [oʊ oʊ oʊ]   speak [oʊ oʊ oʊ] (as in *boat*)

whisper [ɔ ɔ ɔ]   speak [ɔ ɔ ɔ] (as in *bought*)

whisper [ɑ ɑ ɑ]   speak [ɑ ɑ ɑ] (as in *father*)

[ɔ]

[ɑ]

Exercises

The back vowel [u] as in *b**oo**t*

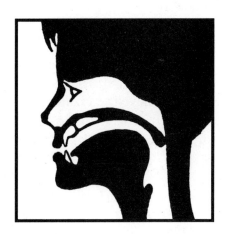

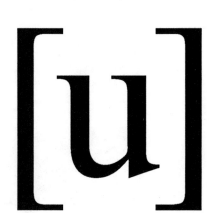

Description

Tongue

The high point of the tongue is in the back of the mouth close to the soft palate. The tip of the tongue touches the back of the bottom front teeth.

Jaw

Relaxed, slightly lowered.

Lips

Very rounded.

Soft Palate

Raised, closing off the nasal passageway.

Common Problems

Insufficient lip rounding. This is a major problem with beginning singers. The [u] requires the most rounded lips of all back vowels.

The insertion of *uh* [ə] between *o͞o* [u] and [l], saying *coo-uhl* [kuəl] for *cool.*

A. Practice the [u] sound.

Read aloud these sounds.

[bu]   [pu]   [bu]   [pu]
[up]   [ub]   [up]   [ub]

Read aloud these English words using [u].

[tul]   [but]   [kup]   [sun]
[mun]   [tun]   [spun]   [krun]

Read aloud these paired words. Do not insert *uh* [ə] between [u] and [l] in the words in the second column.

who	who'll
too	tool
goof	ghoul
stoop	stool
pooch	pool
kook	cool
droop	drool
food	fool
spoon	spool
roost	rule

Read aloud these nonsense words using [u].

[tuk]   [fuf]   [vuz]   [zuk]

B. Transcribe these words into IPA symbols: Each word contains the [u] vowel.

1. boost [bust]   9. two _____

2. crude _____   10. group _____

3. soup _____   11. proof _____

4. cuckoo _____   12. fruit _____

5. Luke _____   13. noon _____

6. spoon _____   14. rude _____

7. blue _____   15. cool _____

8. too _____   16. prune _____

C. Transcribe these IPA symbols into English words.

1. [bun] _____   6. [kluz] _____

2. [tum] _____   7. [pul] _____

3. [luz] _____   8. [brud] _____

4. [fud] _____   9. [glu] _____

5. [drup] _____   10. [mud] _____

D. Transcribe these IPA symbols of nonsense words into orthographic spellings.

1. ['teɪ ˌku] _____   4. ['mɛ ˌnup] _____

2. [plud] _____   5. ['lu ˌvɪ] _____

3. [ˌvi 'tum] _____   6. [ˌɹu 'ku] _____

E. Vocalize using the [u] vowel. Be sure to use sufficient rounding of your lips. This vowel requires the most lip rounding of all back vowels.

two	tool	rude	rule
bloom	you	noon	doom
spoon	move	food	fool

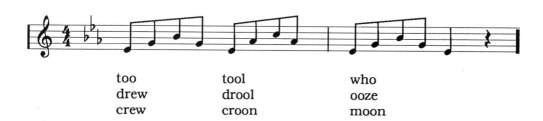

too	tool	who
drew	drool	ooze
crew	croon	moon

Exercises

The back vowel [ʊ] as in b<u>oo</u>k

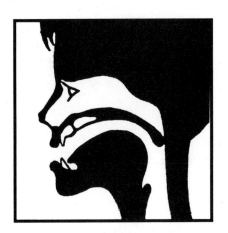

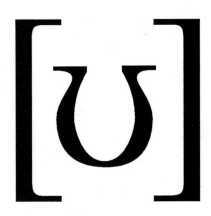

Description

Tongue

The high point of the tongue is in the back of the mouth close to the soft palate. The tip of the tongue touches the back of the bottom front teeth.

Jaw

Slightly lower for [ʊ] than for [u].

Lips

Rounded, but more lax than [u].

Soft Palate

Raised, closing off the nasal passageway.

Common Problems

The substitution of [u] as in *boot* for [ʊ] as in *book*.

The substitution of *uh* [ʌ] for *o͝o* [ʊ].

The insertion of *uh* [ə] or *ih* [ɪ] between [ʊ] and a following consonant. For example, pronouncing the word *put* as [pʊət] or [pʊɪt].

A. Practice the [ʊ] sound.

Read aloud these paired words containing o̅o̅ [u] and ŏŏ [ʊ] to clarify the sound of [ʊ].

[u]	[ʊ]
pool	pull
fool	full
cooed	could
stoop	stood
Luke	look
boost	bush
goo	good
who'd	hood
wooed	wood

Read aloud these paired words to contrast the sound of ŏŏ [ʊ] and *uh* [ʌ].

[ʊ]	[ʌ]
book	buck
hood	hud
took	tuck
look	luck
put	putt

Many Americans are not aware of the [ʊ] sound in their language and often substitute other vowels: uh [ʌ] or o̅o̅ [u].

Read aloud these sounds.

[bʊ] [pʊ] [bʊ] [pʊ]
[ʊp] [ʊb] [ʊp] [ʊb]

Read aloud these English words using [ʊ].

[wʊl] [hʊf] [brʊk] [gʊd]

Read aloud these nonsense words using [ʊ].

[lʊd] [wʊt] ['ʊ ˌpɛt] [plʊd]

B. Transcribe these words into IPA symbols. Each word uses the [ʊ] vowel.

1. bull   [bʊl]   6. took _____

2. put _____   7. hook _____

3. could _____   8. book _____

4. wolf _____   9. hood _____

5. foot _____   10. wool _____

C. Transcribe these words into IPA symbols. These words contain [u] and [ʊ] vowels.

1. flew _____   6. Luke _____

2. full _____   7. look _____

3. stool _____   8. wooed _____

4. stood _____   9. wood _____

5. boom _____   10. mood _____

D. Transcribe these IPA symbols using [u] and [ʊ] into English words.

1. [pruv] _____   5. [pʊl] _____

2. [kʊk] _____   6. [tuts] _____

3. [sun] _____   7. [bʊk] _____

4. [bʊl] _____   8. [gruv] _____

E. Transcribe these IPA symbols of nonsense words into orthographic spellings.

1. [nʊs] _____   3. [lʊp] _____

2. [bʊnd] _____   4. [tʊz] _____

F. Vocalize using [u] and [ʊ] vowels.

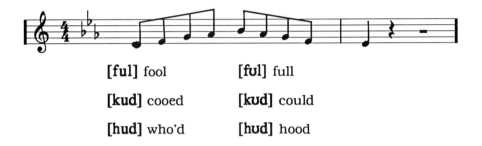

[ful] fool   [fʊl] full

[kud] cooed   [kʊd] could

[hud] who'd   [hʊd] hood

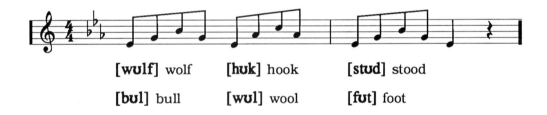

[wʊlf] wolf   [hʊk] hook   [stʊd] stood

[bʊl] bull   [wʊl] wool   [fʊt] foot

Exercises

The pure back vowel [o] as in *pill<u>ow</u>*
and the diphthong [oʊ] as in *b<u>oa</u>t*

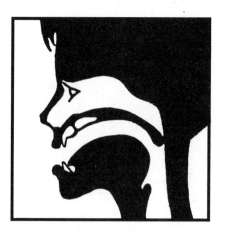

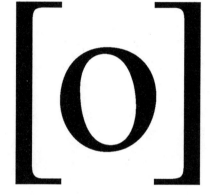

Description

The pure **[o]** vowel as in *pillow* is rarely used in American English, although it may occasionally be found in unstressed syllables.

In American English diphthongal **[oʊ]** is consistently used in place of pure **[o]** and may be considered an allophone of **[o]**.

Tongue

For pure **[o]**, the back of the tongue is elevated toward the mid-back roof of the mouth, but less raised than for **[ʊ]**. The tip of the tongue touches the bottom front teeth.

For diphthongal **[oʊ]**, as the pure **[o]** is released there is a greater rounding of the lips and a quick upward movement of the back of the tongue for the glide **[ʊ]**, thus creating the diphthong.

Jaw

Slightly lower for **[o]** than for **[ʊ]**.

Lips

Rounded.

Soft Palate

Raised, closing off the nasal passageway.

Common Problems

Insufficient lip rounding.

The substitution of diphthongal [oʊ] in foreign languages for pure [o].

The insertion of *uh* [ə] after [ʊ] when followed by a consonant, particularly [n] and [l]. *Bone* becomes *bo-uhn* [boʊ ən].

Pulling the high point of the tongue too far toward the center of the mouth with the result that [oʊ] sounds almost like *uh* [ʌ]. The word *comb* sounds something like *come*.

In Chapter 4, there was a discussion of the diphthong [eɪ]. The same principles apply to [oʊ].

To bring the production of the diphthong [oʊ] into your awareness, speak the word *hoe* aloud in slow motion to notice the movement of your lips and tongue. You should be able to tell that your lips become more rounded as the sound progresses from [o] to [ʊ]. The back of the tongue also moves upward from [o]. You may be less conscious of this movement, because it is so slight. It is easily seen in X-ray images.

Native speakers of English so consistently use diphthongal [oʊ] instead of pure [o] that many have difficulty distinguishing the difference between the two sounds. They hear diphthongal [oʊ] as an indivisible unit which they identify as the pure vowel [o]. Read aloud these words. Feel the lip rounding and the gliding movement of the tongue which occurs from [o] to [ʊ] to produce the diphthong [oʊ].

code, known, home, whole, no, nose, note.

To isolate the pure [o] sound try speaking the word *hoe* in slow motion *without* moving the lips or tongue. The word will sound incomplete and strange to an American. Without the gliding movement, you will produce a pure [o].

Because of the consistent use of diphthongal [oʊ] in place of pure [o] by most Americans, many phoneticians consider [oʊ] as an *allophone* of the phoneme [o]. Kenyon and Knott in A Pronouncing Dictionary of American English, for instance, choose to use the symbol [o] to represent [oʊ].

	This text	Kenyon and Knott
home	[hoʊm]	[hom]
boat	[boʊt]	[bot]
taupe	[toʊp]	[top]
bone	[boʊn]	[bon]

This manual, The IPA for Singers, uses the symbol [oʊ] instead of [o] in transcribing words for two reasons. First, foreign languages use [o] and *do not* use diphthongal [oʊ]. Singers must learn to differentiate between the two sounds. Secondly, in English, the way a singer handles the diphthong is important for stylistic singing.

Just like the diphthong [eɪ], when singing [oʊ] in bel canto or classical music, the pure [o] is sustained until the sound is released. At that moment a quick, short glide to [ʊ] is made. Popular music often approaches the diphthong differently, lengthening the gliding movement, giving more duration to the second vowel [ʊ].

In classical music	sing the word *go*	[go ---------------------------- ʊ]
	sing the word *home*	[ho ------------------------- ʊm]
In popular music	you may sing *go*	[goʊ ---------------------------]
	you may sing *home*	[hoʊ ------------------------- m]

A. Practice the diphthongal [oʊ] sound.

Read aloud these sounds.

[boʊ]	[poʊ]	[boʊ]	[poʊ]
[oʊb]	[oʊp]	[oʊb]	[oʊp]

Read aloud these words containing [oʊ]. Pay attention to the sound of the diphthong [oʊ] being sure to use adequate lip rounding.

hoe	dough
row	door
know	sew
oh	tote
toe	own

Read aloud these words to contrast [oʊ] and *uh* [ʌ].

[oʊ]	[ʌ]
comb	come
mode	mud
known	none
goal	gull

Read aloud these paired words to avoid the insertion of *uh* [ə] between [oʊ] and final consonant. Both lists use the vowel [oʊ].

Joe	Joan
blow	blown
show	shown
foe	phone
woe	won't
boat	bowl
go	goal
show	shoal

Read aloud these nonsense words using [oʊ].

[koʊz]   [moʊk]   [goʊp]

B. Practice these pure [o] sounds.

Read aloud these sounds.

[po]	[bo]	[po]	[bo]
[to]	[do]	[to]	[do]
[o]	[o]	[o]	[o]

English words occasionally use pure [o] in unstressed syllables. Read aloud these words.

obey	[o 'beɪ]
pillow	['pɪ lo]
hollow	['hɑ lo]
potato	[pə 'teɪ to]
proceed	[pro 'sid]

Read aloud these sounds to contrast the pronunciation of pure [o] and diphthongal [oʊ].

[boʊ poʊ]   [boʊ poʊ]   [bo po]   [bo po]
[boʊ bo bo bo boʊ]
[poʊ po po po poʊ]

Read aloud these nonsense words using pure [o].

['to ˌto]   [lov]   [zod]   [sog]

Read aloud these French words using pure [o].

a. beau	[bo]	(beautiful)
b. rôle	[rol]	(role)
c. galop	[ga lo]	(gallop)
d. haut	[o]	(high)

Read aloud these German words using pure [o].

a.	Boot	[boːt]	(boat)
b.	Sohn	[zoːn]	(son)
c.	wo	[voː]	(where)
d.	Mond	[moːnt]	(moon)

Read aloud these Italian words using pure [o].

a.	morale	[mo ˈra lɛ]	(morale)
b.	fonte	[ˈfon tɛ]	(fountain)
c.	bocca	[ˈbokːka]	(mouth)
d.	odorose	[o do ˈro zɛ]	(fragrant)

C. Transcribe these English words into IPA symbols. All words use [oʊ].

1. goes   [goʊz]
2. own   _____
3. comb   _____
4. lone   _____
5. node   _____

6. foe   _____
7. moat   _____
8. goat   _____
9. load   _____
10. float   _____

D. Transcribe these IPA symbols into English words. Each of these words uses [oʊ].

1. [noʊz] _____
2. [soʊks] _____
3. [moʊld] _____

4. [moʊd] _____
5. [ˈmoʊst lɪ] _____
6. [boʊst] _____

E. Transcribe these words into IPA symbols. These words contain [u], [ʊ], and [oʊ].

1. cope   _____
2. cool   _____
3. coat   _____
4. cook   _____
5. known   _____

6. no   _____
7. noon   _____
8. nook   _____
9. whole   _____
10. scroll   _____

F. Transcribe these IPA symbols into English words. These words use [u], [ʊ], and [oʊ].

1. [kʊd] _____   6. [wʊd] _____

2. [loʊp] _____   7. [boʊt] _____

3. [lun] _____   8. [fʊt] _____

4. [stoʊn] _____   9. [koʊst] _____

5. [uz] _____   10. [ful] _____

G. Transcribe these IPA symbols of nonsense words into orthographic letters.

1. ['oʊ ˌnu] _____   4. ['zoʊ ˌpoʊ] _____

2. [ˌkʊ 'poʊ] _____   5. ['loʊ ˌdu] _____

3. [foʊg] _____   6. [ˌmu 'doʊ] _____

H. Vocalize, articulating the back vowels [u], [ʊ] and [oʊ] clearly and easily.

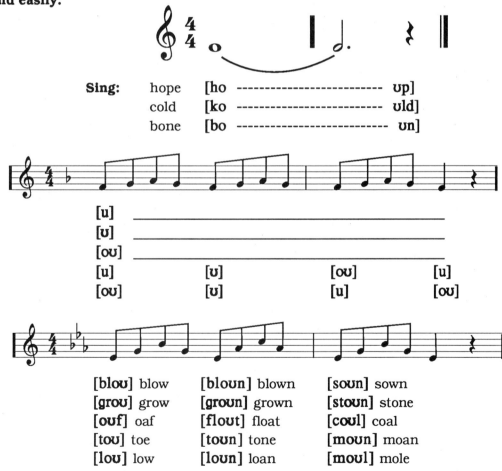

Sing: hope [ho ------------------------- ʊp]
       cold [ko ------------------------- ʊld]
       bone [bo ------------------------- ʊn]

[u] _____
[ʊ] _____
[oʊ] _____

[u]   [ʊ]   [oʊ]   [u]
[oʊ]   [ʊ]   [u]   [oʊ]

[bloʊ] blow   [bloʊn] blown   [soʊn] sown
[groʊ] grow   [groʊn] grown   [stoʊn] stone
[oʊf] oaf   [floʊt] float   [coʊl] coal
[toʊ] toe   [toʊn] tone   [moʊn] moan
[loʊ] low   [loʊn] loan   [moʊl] mole

Exercises

The back vowel [ɔ] as in _awe_

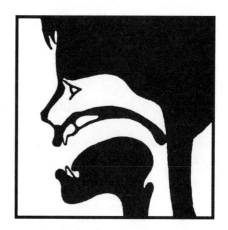

Description

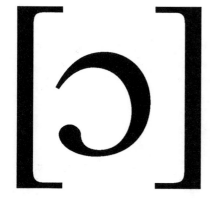

Tongue

The back of the tongue is slightly raised toward the roof of the mouth, but not as high as for [o]. The tip of the tongue touches the back of the bottom front teeth.

Jaw

Lower for [ɔ] than for [o].

Lips

Rounded.

Soft Palate

Raised, closing off the nasal passageway.

Common Problems

Inadequate lowering of the jaw.

Inadequate lip rounding.

The substitution of _oh_ [oʊ] for _aw_ [ɔ].

The substitution of _ah_ [ɑ] for _aw_ [ɔ].

The _aw_ [ɔ] sound confuses many students. They fail to discriminate _aw_ [ɔ] from the sounds immediately above and below on the vowel chart, the back vowels _oh_ [oʊ] and _ah_ [ɑ]. The [ɔ] vowel is ill-formed because of inadequate lip rounding or jaw lowering and results in unclear production of the sound.

To further complicate the matter, some English words have more than one acceptable pronunciation. Depending on the dialect being used, words such as *horrid, office, wash,* or *forest* may be correctly pronounced with *aw* [ɔ], *ah* [ɑ] or with an allophone of *aw* [ɔ], called the *short o* [ɒ].

The *short o* [ɒ] is a sound heard in a British accent, in words like *got, rot, lot,* and *odd.* Typical spellings of the British *short o* [ɒ] are *o* followed by a single consonant in a monosyllable, as in *not,* and by two or more consonants, as in *doll* or *sorrow.* The *short o* [ɒ] can be found on the Vowel Diagram between *aw* [ɔ] and *ah* [ɑ]. See Figure 11.

The *short o* [ɒ] is not universally used in America. The majority of American speakers use *aw* [ɔ] or *ah* [ɑ] for these words. For this reason, *short o* [ɒ] is considered an allophone of both *aw* [ɔ] and *ah* [ɑ].

Figure 11: Vowel Diagram, showing the placement of short o [ɒ].

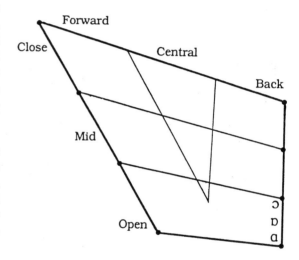

A major characteristic of *short o* [ɒ] is its short duration. Speak these words as if you have a British accent and notice how very brief the vowel sound is: *not, got, lot,* and *odd.* In singing, as vowel sounds are elongated for melodic purposes, the *short o* [ɒ] loses its characteristic shortness and tends to change to *aw* [ɔ] or *ah* [ɑ]. For this reason, this text does not use *short o* in transcriptions.

It is advisable for the teacher to pronounce the word aloud, particularly for testing purposes, so the students can reliably transcribe that pronunciation into IPA symbols. To depend upon a student's personal dialect would make it difficult for a teacher to know whether a mistaken IPA spelling is the result of mis-learning or of an alternate pronunciation choice.

Standard pronunciations can be researched in <u>A</u> <u>Pronouncing</u> <u>Dictionary</u> <u>of</u> <u>American</u> <u>English</u>. The choices in this text follow the General American dialect.

A. Practice the [ɔ] sound.

Read aloud these sounds.

[pɔ] [pɔ] [bɔ] [bɔ]
[ɔb] [ɔb] [ɔp] [ɔp]

Read aloud these words, all of which use [ɔ].

<u>au</u>thors, <u>ya</u>wning, c<u>au</u>sing, ch<u>a</u>lk, distr<u>au</u>ght, c<u>o</u>st, <u>o</u>rchid, <u>a</u>ll, <u>a</u>wed, wr<u>o</u>ng.

Be sure to adequately drop your jaw and round your lips. Insufficient lip rounding is a major failing of beginning singers.

Read aloud these words to contrast [oʊ], [ɔ], and *ah* [ɑ]. Each of these pronunciations is considered standard.

[oʊ]	[ɔ]	[ɑ]
coat	caught	cot
tote	taught	tot
wrote	wrought	rot
ode	awed	odd
pose	pause	pa's
most	moss	ma's

Read aloud these words. The standard pronunciations are given for each word. What is your pronunciation habit?

*Syllables spelled with **w-a-r** are sometimes pronounced with aw [ɔ] and sometimes with ah [ɑ].*

	aw [ɔ]	*ah* [ɑ]
war	[wɔr]	
warn	[wɔrn]	
warp	[wɔrp]	
wart	[wɔrt]	
warrant	[wɔ rənt]	[wɑ rənt]
Warren	[wɔ rən]	[wɑ rən]
warrior	[wɔ rɪ ər]	[wɑ rɪ ər]
warantee	['wɔ rən 'ti]	['wɑ rən 'ti]

Read aloud these nonsense words using [u ʊ oʊ ɔ].

[tup] [tʊp] [toʊs] [tɔz]
[luf] [lʊf] [loʊz] [lɔk]

B. Transcribe these words into IPA symbols. Use [ɔ] for each of these words.

1. saw	[sɔ]	6. horn	_____
2. vault	_____	7. bought	_____
3. cough	_____	8. call	_____
4. sought	_____	9. taught	_____
5. ball	_____	10. stall	_____

C. Transcribe the IPA symbols into English. All the words use [ɔ].

1. [lɔ]	_____	5. [rɔ]	_____
2. [pɔz]	_____	6. ['kɔ fɪn]	_____
3. [tɔk]	_____	7. [ɔ fɪs]	_____
4. [ɔt]	_____	8. [sɔlt]	_____

D. Transcribe these words into IPA symbols. This exercise includes [u ʊ oʊ ɔ].

1. crook _____   6. loose _____

2. fault _____   7. roam _____

3. spoon _____   8. wall _____

4. gnaw _____   9. sew _____

5. flow _____   10. flaw _____

E. Transcribe the IPA symbols into English words. This exercise includes [u ʊ oʊ ɔ].

1. [hoʊm] _____   6. [brɔd] _____

2. [lup] _____   7. [groʊn] _____

3. [lɔft] _____   8. [rud] _____

4. [lʊk] _____   9. [bʊl] _____

5. [tɔl] _____   10. [loʊf] _____

F. Transcribe these IPA symbols of nonsense words into orthographic spellings.

1. [pɔm] _____   4. [ˌvɛr ˈnoʊ] _____

2. [ˌrɔ ˈgun] _____   5. [ˈstoʊ ˌloʊ] _____

3. [ˈlɔ ˌmi] _____   6. [ˈlæ ˌpoʊ] _____

G. Vocalize using back vowels. Maintain vowel integrity as you sing.

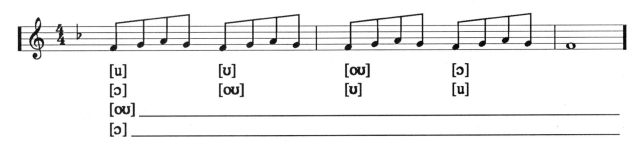

[u]	[ʊ]	[oʊ]	[ɔ]
[ɔ]	[oʊ]	[ʊ]	[u]
[oʊ]	_____
[ɔ]	_____

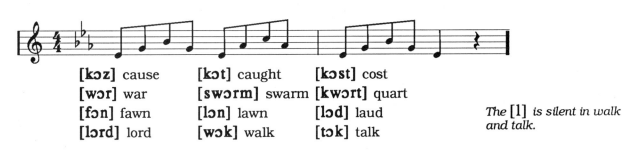

[kɔz] cause   [kɔt] caught   [kɔst] cost

[wɔr] war   [swɔrm] swarm   [kwɔrt] quart

[fɔn] fawn   [lɔn] lawn   [lɔd] laud

[lɔrd] lord   [wɔk] walk   [tɔk] talk

The [l] is silent in walk and talk.

Exercises

The back vowel [ɑ] as in _ah_ or _father_

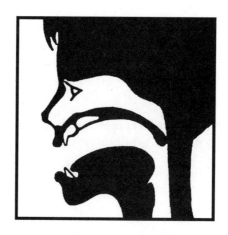

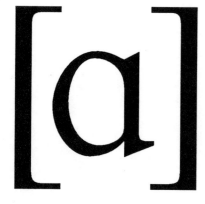

Description

Tongue

The body of the tongue is in a low position for this open back vowel. The tip of the tongue touches the back of the bottom teeth.

Jaw

Relaxed and dropped to its lowest position.

Lips

Open, oval position, neither rounded nor spread horizontally into a smile.

Soft Palate

Raised, closing off the nasal passageway.

Common Problems

Insufficient lowering of the jaw.

Spreading the lips, as in a grin.

Retracting the body of the tongue. Bunching up the tongue by pulling the tip back into the center of the mouth.

The substitution of _bright ah_ **[a]** for **[ɑ]**.

The substitution of _aw_ **[ɔ]** for **[ɑ]**.

The substitution of _uh_ **[ʌ]** for **[ɑ]**.

The substitution of _ǎ_ **[æ]** for **[ɑ]**.

The substitution of the allophone _short o_ **[ɒ]** for **[ɑ]**. The use of this variant is acceptable providing it does not impair clarity.

There are two important articulation cautions for the vowel *ah* [ɑ]. One is to avoid retracting the body of the tongue or pulling the tip of the tongue back away from the back of the bottom front teeth. When the tongue is bunched up in the center of the mouth, the *ah* [ɑ] vowel becomes distorted.

The other caution is to keep the jaw adequately relaxed and lowered. Many speakers and singers hold their teeth too close together, almost in a clenched position. Because of long-standing contrary habits, some students will feel that they are excessively opening the mouth when they produce [ɑ] with a sufficiently dropped jaw.

The tight tongue and jaw are conditions that adversely affect the enunciation clarity of *ah* [ɑ]. Unfortunately, when singers seek a clearer understanding of the *ah* [a] sound, they discover that it is more difficult to find a key word which has a consistent pronunciation for *ah* [a] than for any other English vowel. Even the word *father*, which is commonly used in diction texts, has differing pronunciations. For many people the exclamation *Ah!* becomes a good guide.

A. *Practice the* [ɑ] *sound.*

Read aloud these sounds.

[bɑ] [pɑ] [bɑ] [pɑ]
[ab] [ap] [ab] [ap]
[mɑ] [mɑ] [mɑ] [mɑ]

Be careful not to nasalize [ɑ] *in the syllable* [mɑ].

Read aloud these words containing *ah* [ɑ].

ah	option
obstinate	colossal
odd	prompt
yacht	jock
toxic	opposite
box	cobbler
squash	blonde
ominous	mob
job	oxen

Read aloud these words which use both [ɑ] and [ɔ].

Some of the following words are pronounced in more than one way. The IPA transcriptions beside the words indicate their standard pronunciations. Read across the page, saying the words with both of their optional pronunciations. Do you use *ah* [ɑ] or *aw* [ɔ] for these words in your normal dialect?

	[ɑ]	[ɔ]
horrid	[ˈhɑ rɪd]	[ˈhɔ rɪd]
office	[ˈɑ fɪs]	[ˈɔ fɪs]
doll	[dɑl]	[dɔl]
sorrow	[ˈsɑ ro]	[ˈsɔ ro]
wash	[wɑʃ]	[wɔʃ]
coffee	[ˈkɑ fɪ]	[ˈkɔ fɪ]

If you find that there are inconsistencies in your pronunciations in the preceding list, you might want to check A Pronouncing Dictionary of American English to be sure that you are using standard pronunciations. If you heard a variation from the *ah* [ɑ] and *aw* [ɔ] pronunciations suggested above, it may be that you are using the alternate allophone called the *short o* [ɒ], which was discussed previously in the exercise for *aw* [ɔ].

Read aloud the following words using the General American *ah* [ɑ] on each word. The substitution of the forward *bright ah* [a] for the *back ah* [ɑ] occurs frequently in words in standard New England dialect, but it is preferable to use General American speech for classical singing.

farm	[fɑrm]
barn	[bɑrn]
car	[kɑr]
calm	[kɑm]
alms	[ɑmz]
park	[pɑrk]

Read these words aloud. Read across the page to contrast the sounds of *ah* [ɑ], *aw* [ɔ] and *oh* [oʊ]. Clarify each sound by being precise in your articulation.

Caution: Many speakers mis-articulate the open [ɑ] by closing and rounding which results in the vowel [ɔ] or even the more close [oʊ]. This distortion occurs in words where *a* is followed by an *r*. Be careful that the word *star* does not become *store*, and that *heart* does not become *hort*.

[ɑ]	[ɔ]	[oʊ]
ah	awe	owe
star	stall	stone
far	for	four
Don	dawn	dote
box	bought	boat
car	cough	coat
top	taught	tote
lard	lord	load
ardor	order	odor
stark	stork	stoke

Read aloud these sounds. Start with a fully dropped, relaxed jaw for *ah* [ɑ]. Feel the movements of the lips, jaw and tongue as you go from one sound to the next.

[ɑ ɔ oʊ ɔ ɑ]

[ɑ ɔ oʊ ɔ ɑ]

[ɑ ɔ oʊ ɔ ɑ]

Read aloud these words to contrast [ɑ] and *uh* [ʌ]. Be sure to lower your jaw sufficiently, so that you do not substitute *uh* [ʌ] for [ɑ].

[ɑ]	[ʌ]
rot	rut
balm	bum
fond	fund
shock	shuck
lock	luck
psalm	some

Some people bring the tongue into a position which is too forward and raised when saying [ɑ]. This results in a sound something like ă [æ] (as in *bat*). The word *stop* begins to sound like *stap* [stæp]. Clarify the difference in articulation between the two open vowels [ɑ] and [æ] by alternately saying the two vowels. Feel the up and down movement of the tongue as you read aloud [æ ɑ æ ɑ æ ɑ]. Keep your jaw lowered and the tongue down for the vowel [ɑ] in words like: *alms, are, ark, arbor, otter, ox,* and *opposite*.

In foreign languages it is important to contrast the sound of the open forward bright ah [a] and the open back dark ah [ɑ].

Read aloud these vowel sounds, alternating between *bright* and *dark ah*. Feel the movement of the tongue as it moves more forward and up for *bright ah* [a] and down and back for *dark ah* [ɑ]. Keep your jaw dropped to a low, relaxed position for both vowels.

[a ɑ a ɑ a]

[a ɑ a ɑ a]

[a ɑ a ɑ a]

B. Transcribe these words into IPA symbols. Each word uses [ɑ].

The l is silent in calm [kɑm], balm, palm and psalm.

1. calm   [kɑm]   10. fond   _____
2. balm   _____   11. lock   _____
3. quality _____   12. psalm   _____
4. palm   _____   13. top   _____
5. pop   _____   14. rot   _____
6. stop   _____   15. ah   _____
7. god   _____   16. spots   _____
8. mop   _____   17. barn   _____
9. mom   _____   18. Don   _____

C. Transcribe these IPA symbols into English words.

1. [kɑp] _____   3. [hɑrd] _____
2. [kɑd] _____   4. [hɑk] _____

D. Transcribe these IPA symbols of nonsense words into orthographic spellings.

    1. ['lɑ ˌku] _____   3. [ˌgɑ 'gun] _____

    2. [ˌzɑ 'bɑ] _____   4. ['di ˌdɑ] _____

E. Vocalize using back vowels.

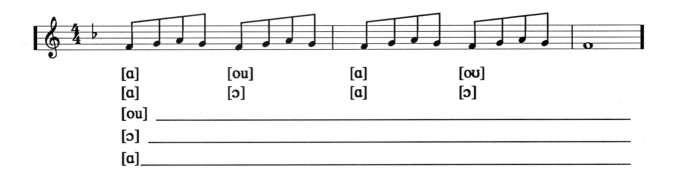

    [ɑ]   [ou]   [ɑ]   [ou]

    [ɑ]   [ɔ]   [ɑ]   [ɔ]

    [ou] _____

    [ɔ] _____

    [ɑ] _____

[oud] ode	[ɔd] awed	[ɑd] odd
[tout] tote	[tɔt] taught	[tɑt] tot
[nout] note	[nɔt] naught	[nɑt] not
[rout] wrote	[rɔt] wrought	[rɑt] rot
[bout] boat	[bɔt] bought	[bɑks] box

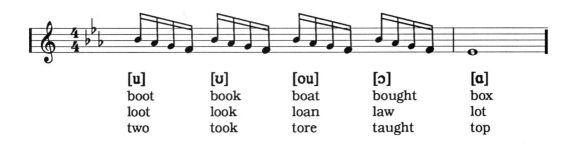

[u]	[ʊ]	[ou]	[ɔ]	[ɑ]
boot	book	boat	bought	box
loot	look	loan	law	lot
two	took	tore	taught	top

Chapter 5 Worksheet 1

Transcribe these words into IPA symbols.
These words use back vowels.

1. pork	[pɔrk]	16. rogue	[roʊg]
2. mall	[mɔl]	17. spoon	[spun]
3. swap	[swap]	18. stock	[stak]
4. star	[star]	19. stood	[stʊd]
5. hook	[hʊk]	20. caught	[kat]
6. doe	[doʊ]	21. pothole	[pat hoʊl]
7. bond	[band]	22. spore	[spɔr]
8. monsoon	[man 'sun]	23. prose	[proʊz]
9. got	[gat]	24. hook	[hʊk]
10. stomp	[stamp]	25. tall	[tɔl]
11. sod	[sad]	26. cross	[krɔs]
12. photo	['foʊtoʊ]	27. store	[stɔr]
13. spot	[spat]	28. moose	[mus]
14. gold	[goʊld]	29. pull	[pʊl]
15. ore	[ɔr]	30. call	[kɔl]

Transcribe these IPA symbols into English words.

1. [dɔg]	dog	11. [trus]	truce
2. [drɔ]	draw	12. [sʊt]	soot
3. [wɑnt]	want	13. [huz]	whose
4. [mut]		14. [roʊd]	road
5. ['goʊ ri]		15. [roʊl]	roll
6. [soʊrs]	sewers	16. [rul]	rule
7. [tut]	toot	17. [rɑk]	rock
8. [mɑp]	mop	18. [ɔft]	oft
9. [moʊp]	mope	19. [mɔrg]	
10. [mɔs]	moss	20. [oʊt]	oat

Chapter 5 Worksheet 2

Transcribe these words into IPA symbols.
These words use back vowels.

1. spool   [spul]
2. posy   [pozi]
3. pawed   [pɔd]
4. trough   [trɔf]
5. oboe   [oʊboʊ]

6. flu   [flu]
7. taut   [tɔt]
8. grotto   [gratoʊ]
9. waltz   [wɔlts]
10. frost   [frɔst]

11. blown   [bloʊn]
12. malt   [mɔlt]
13. far   [far]
14. for   [fɔr]
15. fore   [fɔr]

16. lost   [lɔst]
17. low   [loʊ]
18. soft   [saft]
19. golf   [galf]
20. cork   [kɔrk]

21. war   [wɔr]
22. wart   [wɔrt]
23. warp   [wɔrp]
24. carp   [karp]
25. cord   [kɔrd]

26. squall   [skwɔl]
27. tarp   [tarp]
28. form   [fɔrm]
29. farm   [farm]
30. too   [tu]

Transcribe these IPA symbols into English words.

1. [gʊd] good
2. [spa] spa
3. [moʊr] more
4. [noʊn] noun
5. [kʊk] cook
6. [bɔs] boss
7. [groʊn] grown
8. [cad] cod
9. [loʊm] loam
10. [blum] bloom

11. [zum] zoom
12. [plap] plop
13. [bɔt] bought
14. [stoʊn] stone
15. [hu] who
16. [tʊk] took
17. [koʊm] comb
18. [smak] smock
19. [kʊd] could
20. [krʊks] crooks

Chapter 5 Worksheet 3

Transcribe these words into IPA symbols.
These words contain forward and back vowels.

1. Pluto	[plutou]	16. plutonic	[plutɑnɪk]
2. pussyfoot	[pusifʊt]	17. obese	[oubis]
3. evolve	[ɪvɑlv]	18. brook	[brʊk]
4. fought	[fɔt]	19. loop	[lup]
5. robin	[rɑbən]	20. caustic	[kɑstɪk]
6. walk	[wɔk]	21. story	[stɔri]
7. rookie	[rʊki]	22. Oz	[ɑz]
8. truly	[truli]	23. bullet	[bʊlət]
9. scolded	[skouldəd]	24. clause	[klɔz]
10. gnome	[noʊm]	25. pulpit	[pʊlpɪt]
11. garlic	[gɑrlɪk]	26. scald	[skɔld]
12. manhood	[mænhʊd]	27. scoot	[skut]
13. plaudit	[plɔdɪt]	28. rocket	[rɑkət]
14. caulk	[kɑk]	29. cruise	[kruz]
15. doomsday	[dumzdei]	30. causeway	[kɑzwei]

Transcribe these IPA symbols into English words.

1. [skroʊl]	scroll	11. [tʊr]	
2. ['bɑ dɪ]	body	12. [brud]	brood
3. ['ɔn ˌsɛt]	onset	13. [poʊst]	post
4. [gus]	goose	14. [brʊm]	
5. ['kʊ kɪ]	cook	15. ['hoʊ lɪ]	holy
6. ['hɑ lɪ]	holy	16. ['sɑ lɪd]	salad
7. ['tɑr dɪ]	tardy	17. [hut]	hoot
8. ['bloʊ tɪd]	bloated	18. ['koʊ zɪ]	cozy
9. [ɔf]	off	19. [rʊk]	rook
10. [bum]	boom	20. [smoʊk]	smoke

CHAPTER 6
CENTRAL VOWELS

Introduction to Central Vowels

The central vowels in English are those vowels which are produced with the high point of the tongue centrally located in the mouth. Although there are several IPA symbols for the central vowels, they represent only two basic sounds: *uh* as in *up* and *ûr* as in *burr*. Each central vowel has a specific relationship to stress within a word; therefore, before listing the symbols for the central vowels, this chapter will present a discussion of stressing and unstressing in English.

Stressing and Unstressing

Stressing and unstressing in the English language is a phenomenon which influences both the pronunciation of the word and its IPA transcription. The term *stress* refers to the varying degrees of emphasis in a word. Stress occurs when a speaker changes the loudness, duration or pitch of a particular syllable. In unstressed syllables, the degree of emphasis is changed by altering the vowel itself.

There are three levels of stress in English words. *Primary* stress refers to the syllable having the strongest emphasis within a word; *secondary* stress refers to a syllable with medium emphasis; and *unstressing* refers to the syllable with the shortest and weakest stress.

Using the word *secretary* ['sɛ krə ˌtɛ rɪ] as an example, we would find primary stress on the first syllable, s̲e̲c̲retary; secondary stress on the third syllable, secret̲a̲r̲y; and unstressing on the remaining syllables, sec̲r̲e̲t̲a̲r̲y̲.

Primary and secondary stressed syllables are indicated in IPA by small marks located before the syllable. The word *handsaw* would be written ['hænd ˌsɔ] with the primary stress mark *above* and *before* the syllable and the secondary stress mark *below* and *before* the syllable. Refer to Chapter 2, Helpful Hints for Using IPA, for further discussion for reading stress in IPA.

Occasionally, the pure [e] as in **chaotic** *[ke 'ɑ tɪk] and the pure [o] as in the word* **pillow** *['pɪ lo] are used in unstressed syllables. However, this is rare.*

In unstressed syllables, the American speaker actually changes the stressed vowel to an indistinct, brief *uh* or *ih.* (The symbol for the brief *uh* sound is [ə], known as *schwa.*) For example, the second syllable of the word *breakfast* ['brɛk ˌfəst] is pronounced with *schwa* [ə]. It is not pronounced with the sound of *ă* [æ] as in *fast, break-fast* ['brɛk ˌfæst]. An example of using the unstressed *ih* [ɪ] would be in the word *added* ['æ dɪd].

If an unstressed vowel is incorrectly stressed, the excessive stressing will not only change the rhythm of the word, it will typically change the vowel back to its stressed sound and will distort the pronunciation of the word, as happens when incorrectly stressing the first syllable of *po-lice* ['poʊ lis] instead of stressing the second syllable *po-lice* [pə'lis].

It is important to pay close attention to the stressing and unstressing of a word in singing, as it is in speech. Unstressed syllables in music often have great loudness and long duration, resulting in a tendency to sing the stressed version of the vowel sound. Being aware of the stressing and unstressing of a word will help you find the appropriate vowel sound to sing.

There are times, of course, when speakers or singers wish to give special emphasis to an unstressed syllable. For instance, the word *exalt* [ɪg 'zɔlt] is normally pronounced with an unstressed *ih* [ɪ] in the first syllable. To give the word dramatic emphasis, the speaker may convincingly say *ex-alt!* [ˌɛg 'zɔlt] bringing the *ih* [ɪ] back to an *eh* [ɛ]. If this is done occasionally in moments of intense emotion, it can be expressive. However, if stressing of this nature is done repeatedly, the result is *over-stressing* and the singing will sound pretentious and weighty. Opera singers do this often enough that they are satirized for it. Avoid over-stressing in your singing by giving thoughtful attention to unstressing when singing in English.

Read aloud these words. Notice how the unstressed vowels *schwa* [ə] and *ih* [ɪ] are used. In some unstressed syllables, either *schwa* [ə] or *ih* [ɪ] can be used. In some words, there is only one choice of unstressed vowel.

Dall<u>a</u>s	['dæ ləs]	['dæ lɪs]
lett<u>u</u>ce	['lɛ təs]	['lɛ tɪs]
beaut<u>i</u>ful	['bju tə fəl]	['bju tɪ fəl]
anal<u>ysi</u>s	[ə 'næ lə səs]	[ə 'næ lɪ sɪs]
<u>a</u>bove	[ə 'bʌv]	
<u>o</u>ppose	[ə 'pouz]	
dem<u>o</u>n	['di mən]	
bell<u>y</u>		['bɛ lɪ]
pall<u>i</u>d		['pæ lɪd]
go<u>i</u>ng		['gou ɪŋ]

Stress in Foreign Languages

Every language has its own sounds and its own patterns for stressing. In French, for instance, stress is achieved by giving vowels longer duration rather than greater loudness as in English, and the weak sound of *schwa* [ə] becomes more close and rounded, almost like an *umlauted o* [ø] (see Chapter 15). In Italian, the phenomenon of unstressing does not exist and *schwa* [ə] is never used.

One of the greatest pitfalls for Americans who sing in foreign languages, is the tendency to use the ill-defined, brief *schwa* [ə] too often. Their English diction habits of stress and unstressing inappropriately spill over into their foreign diction. The patterns of stress in each language must be carefully observed by singers in order to achieve the flavor and flow of that language.

Description of the Central Vowels

The symbols for the central vowels in English are paired in the study of phonetics according to their relationship with stressing and unstressing. The positions of the tongue during the production of each of the central vowels are illustrated in the diagram on the right.

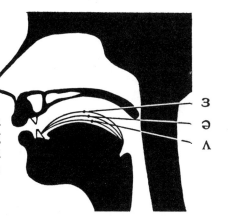

ɜ
ə
ʌ

The *uh* sounds [ʌ] and [ə]

The sound of *uh* in English is represented by the two IPA symbols [ʌ] and *schwa* [ə]:

1. The vowel sound *uh* [ʌ] as in *up* [ʌp]. The *uh* [ʌ] symbol is referred to by its sound and is used only in stressed syllables.

2. The vowel sound *schwa* [ə] as in *appeal* [ə 'pil]. This symbol is always referred to by its name, *schwa*, and is used only in unstressed syllables.

Read aloud these words which use stressed *uh* [ʌ].

> c<u>u</u>p
> h<u>u</u>t
> m<u>u</u>tt
> s<u>o</u>me
> c<u>o</u>me
> d<u>u</u>ck

Read aloud these words which use *unstressed schwa* [ə].

> <u>a</u>ware
> <u>a</u>bout
> <u>o</u>ffici<u>a</u>l
> s<u>u</u>ppose
> ev<u>e</u>n
> cru<u>e</u>l

The *ûr* sounds [ɜ] and [ɚ]

The sound of *ûr* as in *b<u>urr</u>* and *butt<u>er</u>* is represented by two IPA symbols, [ɜ] and [ɚ], both of which have small, hook-like marks on the upper part of the symbols. These hook-like marks indicate that a vowel has been blended with the consonant *r* to produce the *r-colored* vowel.

In unstressed syllables, all English vowels can be reduced to schwa [ə], except for ûr [ɜ] which reduces to hooked schwa [ɚ].

1. The vowel sound *ûr* [ɜ], as in *b<u>ur</u>r* [bɜ]. This symbol is referred to by its sound or by the name, *hooked reversed epsilon*. It is used only in stressed syllables. [ɜ] is spelled in English as *ur* as in *<u>ur</u>ge*, *er* as in *h<u>er</u>d*, *ir* as in *b<u>ir</u>d*, *ear* as in *<u>ear</u>th*, *or* as in *w<u>or</u>k*, *our* as in *j<u>our</u>ney*.

2. The vowel sound *ûr* [ɚ], as in *batt<u>er</u>* ['bæ tɚ]. This symbol is referred to by the name *hooked schwa*. It is used only in unstressed syllables and is spelled *er* as in *dimm<u>er</u>*, *or* as in *mot<u>or</u>*, *ar* as in *doll<u>ar</u>*, *ure* as in *pleas<u>ure</u>*, *ur* as in *fem<u>ur</u>*, *yr* as in *zeph<u>yr</u>*, *oar* as in *cupb<u>oar</u>d*.

To produce the r-colored vowels, the tip of the tongue is retracted and suspended in the middle of the mouth. Feel your tongue position and listen to the sound of the vowels in the following words.

Read aloud these words which use *stressed ûr* [ɝ].

burn
her
sir
merge
bird
learn
urn
burst
worth

Read aloud these words which use *hooked schwa* [ɚ].

mother
brother
better
actor
over
hangar
never

The *r-less ûr* sounds [ɜ] and [ə]

In some dialects of the United States, such as the Southern dialect, the ûr sound of English is pronounced *without the r-color*. The IPA represents that *r-less* vowel sound with the two symbols, [ɜ] and *schwa* [ə].

1. The vowel *r-less ûr* [ɜ] is the sound used by Southern speakers who drop their r in words like *bird* [bɜd]. This symbol is referred to as *r-less ûr*, as *reversed epsilon*, or simply by its sound. It is used only in stressed syllables.

2. The *schwa* [ə] is used for the sound of *r-less ûr* in unstressed syllables, as by speakers who drop their r in words like *butter* ['bʌ tə].

To produce *r-less ûr* [ɜ], the tip of the tongue touches the back of the bottom front teeth. The body of the tongue moves into a forward, central position. The lips tend to round slightly. The major articulation contrast between *r-colored ûr* [ɝ] and *r-less ûr* [ɜ] is that the *r-colored ûr* [ɝ] is produced with the tip of the tongue raised and suspended in the center of the mouth and the *r-less ûr* [ɜ] is produced with the tip of the tongue down behind the bottom front teeth.

Experiment with these two sounds. Say one after the other, feeling the movement of the tip of the tongue — up for *ûr* [ɝ] and down behind the teeth for *r-less ûr* [ɜ].

[ɝ]   [ɜ]   [ɝ]   [ɜ]   [ɝ]   [ɜ]

In English, the sound of *r-less ûr* [ɜ] is something like an *uh* [ʌ] produced with half-rounded lips. And if you are familiar with foreign languages, you may recognize that the sound of *r-less ûr* [ɜ] is similar to *umlauted ö* [œ] of German, only with laxer, less rounded lips (see Chapter 15).

Read aloud these words imitating a Southern drawl, using *stressed r-less ûr* [ɜ] and dropping the *r*.

hu<u>r</u>t   [hɜt]
bi<u>r</u>d   [bɜd]
he<u>r</u>d   [hɜd]
le<u>ar</u>n   [lɜn]
<u>ea</u>rn   [ɜn]
tu<u>r</u>n   [tɜn]

Read aloud these words imitating a Southern drawl, using *unstressed schwa* [ə] and dropping the *r*.

butt<u>er</u>   ['bʌ tə]
mot<u>or</u>   ['mou tə]
act<u>or</u>   ['æk tə]
suff<u>er</u>   ['sʌ fə]
doll<u>ar</u>   ['dɑ lə]

Singing with the *ûr* Sounds

The sounds of the *r-colored ûr* [ɝ] and *hooked schwa* [ɚ], being produced with a tense, retracted tongue, result in a singing tone which is more tense and less free than the vibrant, easy tone desired in singing. Many singers, therefore, choose to substitute the *r-less ûr* [ɜ] and *schwa* [ə] for the *r-colored ûr* [ɝ] and *hooked schwa* [ɚ]. When pronouncing a word, the r-value can be added as a consonant, rather than blended with the vowel. Words would then be sung as *herd* [hɜrd], *bird* [bɜrd], *learn* [lɜrn].

Sing these words, sustaining the *r-less ûr* [ɜ] sound until the release of the note.

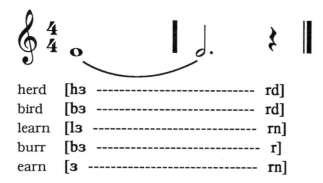

herd	[hɜ	-----------------------------	rd]
bird	[bɜ	-----------------------------	rd]
learn	[lɜ	-----------------------------	rn]
burr	[bɜ	-----------------------------	r]
earn	[ɜ	-----------------------------	rn]

Sing these words, sustaining the *r-less schwa* [ə] in the unstressed syllables.

bearer	[bɛ	---------------	rə	---------	r]
ever	[ɛ	---------------	və	---------	r]
comfort	[kʌ	---------------	mfə	-------	rt]
after	[æ	---------------	ftə	--------	r]
dollar	[dɑ	---------------	lə	---------	r]

Summary

As we approach the exercises for the central vowels, notice how they fall into consistent pairs of sounds relative to stressing and unstressing as shown on the following table.

Stressed	Unstressed
[ʌ]	[ə]
[ɝ]	[ɚ]
[ɜ]	[ə]

The student is encouraged to refer to this table often until it is clear that the vowels in the first column are always used in stressed syllables, while those in the second column are always used in unstressed syllables.

Exercises

The central vowel [ʌ] as in b**u**d

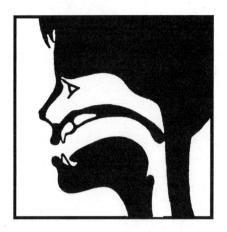

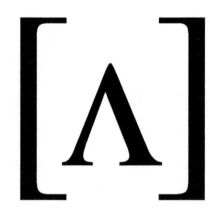

Description

The symbol [ʌ], which represents the sound of *uh*, is used <u>only</u> in syllables of primary or secondary stress.

Tongue

The middle of the tongue is in a low position, slightly arched back of the center of the mouth, which designates [ʌ] as a mid, central vowel. The tip touches the back of the bottom front teeth.

Jaw

In a mid-low position.

Lips

Open and unrounded.

Soft Palate

Raised, closing off the nasal passageway.

Common Problems

The substitution of *ih* [ɪ] or *eh* [ɛ] for *uh* [ʌ], caused by positioning the tongue too high and forward. Example: *just* may sound like *gist* or *jest.*

The substitution of *o͝o* [ʊ] for *uh* [ʌ], caused by pulling the tongue too far back, closing the jaw, or rounding the lips. Example: *love* [lʌv] may sound like [lʊv].

The substitution of *ah* [ɑ] for *uh* [ʌ], caused when the mouth is too open and the tongue is too flat. Example: *love* [lʌv] may sound like [lɑv].

The substitution of *r-less ûr* [ɜ] for *uh* [ʌ], caused by rounding the lips, closing the mouth, or bringing the middle of the tongue forward and up. Example: *mud* [mʌd] may sound like [mɜd].

The nasalization of *uh* [ʌ] when it precedes *m, n,* or *ng,* as in *sun, come, hung.*

In English there are two IPA symbols used to represent the *uh* sound. The symbol [ʌ], presented in this exercise, is used only in primary or secondary stressed syllables. The *schwa* [ə], a similar sound, is used only in unstressed syllables. The two sounds differ because the high point of the tongue for [ʌ] is positioned slightly back of center, contrasted to [ə], which is more centered in the mouth. The vowel [ʌ] is produced with a relaxed, mid-low jaw position and unrounded lips.

As you can see from the previous page under the category Common Problems, there is a long list of substitutions for the vowel *uh* [ʌ]. Speakers often replace *uh* [ʌ] with *ih* [ɪ], *eh* [ɛ], *oo* [ʊ], *ah* [ɑ], or *r-less ûr* [ɜ]! The following lists of words will help you clarify the sound and feeling of *uh* [ʌ].

A. Practice the stressed [ʌ] sound.

Read aloud these sounds.

[bʌ]   [pʌ]   [bʌ]   [pʌ]

[ʌb]   [ʌp]   [ʌb]   [ʌp]

Read aloud these words. Articulate carefully and avoid moving your tongue too far forward, which will produce [ɪ] or [ɛ] or too far backward, which will produce [ʊ]. The vowel sound in each of these words is [ʌ] and should sound the same.

| s<u>u</u>ch | m<u>u</u>ch | s<u>o</u>me | br<u>o</u>ther | l<u>o</u>ve |
| j<u>u</u>st | tr<u>u</u>ck | tr<u>ou</u>ble | d<u>u</u>ck | c<u>o</u>me |

*When [ʌ] precedes a consonant made in the front of the mouth, the tongue can be brought too high and forward in the mouth and will sound like [ɪ] or [ɛ]. A word such as **just** may sound like **jist** or **jest**.*

Read aloud these paired words to contrast the [ɑ] and [ʌ] vowel sounds.

[ɑ]	[ʌ]
hot	hut
bomb	bum
lock	luck
cot	cut
got	gut

Be careful not to pull the tongue too far back and up because it will result in the substitution of o͝o [ʊ] for uh [ʌ].

Read aloud these sounds without pausing between [ɑ] and [ʌ]. Leave the jaw dropped to a low position and feel the movement of the jaw and tongue as you say these sounds. The tongue is flatter for [ɑ] than for [ʌ].

[ɑ ʌ ɑ ʌ ɑ ʌ ɑ ʌ]

If the tongue is too flat in the mouth, the vowel [ɑ] will be sounded instead of [ʌ].

Read aloud these paired words to contrast *uh* [ʌ] with *ûr* [ɝ] as in *burr*. The tip of the tongue touches the back of the bottom front teeth for *uh* [ʌ]. It retracts and raises for *ûr* [ɝ].

[ʌ]	[ɝ]
m<u>u</u>tt	m<u>ur</u>der
l<u>u</u>ck	l<u>ear</u>ner
b<u>u</u>t	b<u>urr</u>
m<u>u</u>d	m<u>er</u>cy
p<u>u</u>tt	p<u>urr</u>
h<u>u</u>t	h<u>er</u>

The uh [ʌ] is a low central vowel. Do not round the lips, close the jaw, or bring the middle of the tongue forward and up. These movements will result in the substitution of r-less ûr [ɝ], for uh [ʌ].

Read aloud these words. Avoid substituting *r-less ûr* [ɝ] for *uh* [ʌ] in the second column. Keep your jaw dropped to a mid-low position and lips unrounded for *uh* [ʌ]. Both columns of words should be pronounced with *uh* [ʌ].

[ʌ]	[ʌ]
m<u>u</u>tt	<u>o</u>ther
l<u>u</u>ck	l<u>o</u>ve
m<u>u</u>d	m<u>o</u>ney
p<u>u</u>tt	p<u>u</u>nish

Read aloud these sounds without pausing between the *uh* [ʌ] and *r-less ûr* [ɝ]. Keep your jaw in a relaxed, low position. Feel the body of the tongue move up and forward and the lips slightly round for the [ɝ]

[ʌ ɝ ʌ ɝ ʌ ɝ ʌ ɝ ʌ]

Read aloud these paired words to avoid nasalization in the words in the second column. All words contain [ʌ].

[ʌ]	[ʌ]
cut	come
such	sun
double	dumb
duck	dump
rut	run
mutt	punt
putt	pump

B. Transcribe these words into IPA symbols. Each word contains [ʌ].

The words one and won are both transcribed the same, [wʌn].

1. pump [pʌmp]   8. sun _____

2. luck _____   9. dug _____

3. from _____   10. cup _____

4. dove _____   11. Bud's _____

5. love _____   12. one _____

6. cut _____   13. won _____

7. up _____   14. dust _____

C. Transcribe these IPA symbols into English words.

1. [fʌnd] _____   6. [bʌk] _____
2. [rʌb] _____   7. [dʌk] _____
3. ['mʌ nɪ] _____   8. ['bʌ dɪ] _____
4. [trʌks] _____   9. [stʌmp] _____
5. [hʌm] _____   10. [mʌd] _____

D. Transcribe these IPA symbols for nonsense words into orthographic spellings.

1. ['dʌ ˌmɛ ˌtu] _____   4. [pɛ 'lʌg] _____
2. [ˌvɛ 'zʌ ˌmɛ] _____   5. ['lʌm ˌsɪ] _____
3. [ˌtɪ 'zʌd] _____   6. [ˌnɛ 'fʌz] _____

E. Vocalize, articulating the [ʌ] vowel clearly and easily.

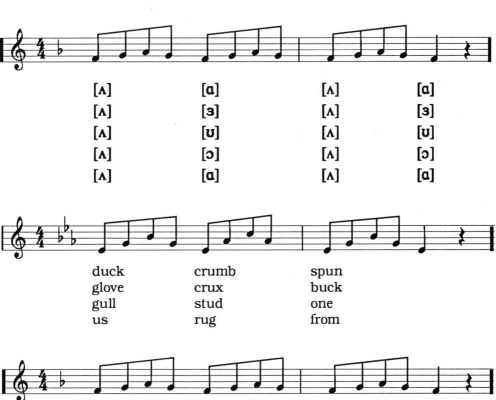

Exercises

The central vowel *schwa* [ə] as in *<u>appeal</u>*

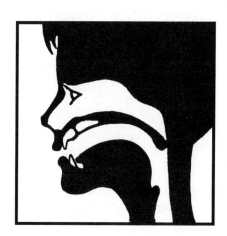

Description

Used only in unstressed syllables, the sound of *schwa* [ə] is a lax and brief *uh*. It is possible to confuse *uh* [ʌ] with *schwa* [ə] when length and stress are disregarded. Because of the brief, ill-defined nature of *schwa* [ə], it cannot be referred to by its sound. We call it *schwa*, a German derivative from a Hebrew word meaning "little" or "weak."

Tongue

The high point of the tongue is located in the center of the mouth, differing from the stressed *uh* [ʌ], which has the high point of the tongue back of center. The tip of the tongue touches the back of the bottom front teeth.

Jaw

Relaxed, slightly dropped.

Lips

The lips are neutral or, on occasions, slightly rounded.

Soft Palate

Raised, closing off the nasal passageway.

Common Problems

The omission of the [ə], particularly between consonants in the middle of a word as in *bakery.*

The substitution of a stressed vowel for *schwa* [ə]. For example, saying *oppress* as [ˌoʊ ˈprɛs] instead of [əˈprɛs].

Schwa [ə] is the most used sound in our language, occurring in most unstressed syllables. Any English vowel may be represented by schwa in an unstressed syllable.

A. Practice the *schwa* [ə] sound.

Read aloud these words to identify the *schwa* [ə] sound.

agree

affair

offend

jewel

variety

sofa

ago

coma

president

Read aloud these words being careful not to omit the *schwa* [ə] sound.

bakery

cabinet

parade

police

jewel

veteran

traveler

funeral

Read aloud these words. The final *le* forms a syllable. It is transcribed as [əl]

litt<u>le</u>	['lɪ təl]
ab<u>le</u>	['eɪ bəl]
app<u>le</u>	['æ pəl]
tab<u>le</u>	['teɪ bəl]
cab<u>le</u>	['keɪ bəl]

B. Transcribe these words into IPA symbols. Each words contains a *schwa* [ə].

1. bottle	['ba təl]	11. aware	[ə wɛr]
2. sodium	['sɔ di əm]	12. symbol	[
3. adapt	[ə'd æp t]	13. ado	. [ə d u]
4. affair	[ə f	14. battery	
5. suppose	[sə'p o z]	15. mystery	
6. again	[ə'g ɛ n]	16. away	
7. consistent	[kən'si tənt]	17. camera	
8. rubble	['r ʌ bəl]	18. cruel	
9. tumble	['t ʌ m bəl]	19. comma	
10. president		20. period	

C. Transcribe these IPA symbols into English words.

1. ['dʌ bəl]		7. ['sɛn trəl]	
2. ['sɛ krə ˌtɛ rɪ]		8. [ɪg 'zæm pəl]	
3. [ə 'doʊr]		9. ['sʌ dən]	
4. ['æ lə ˌfoʊn]		10. [ə 'drɛs]	
5. ['gæ lə rɪ]		11. ['oʊ pən]	
6. ['dɪ fə rənt]		12. ['mʌ fəld]	

D. Transcribe these nonsense words into IPA symbols.

1. [zə 'mi nə] _____   3. [prə 'du kə] _____

2. ['kloʊ tə mə] _____   4. ['krɑ də ˌseɪ rə] _____

E. Vocalize, articulating the *schwa* [ə] clearly and easily.

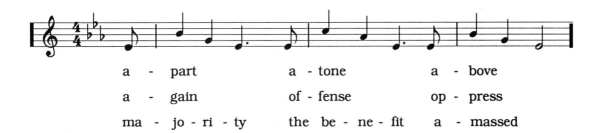

a	-	part	a	-	tone	a	-	bove

a   -   part   a - tone   a - bove

a   -   gain   of - fense   op - press

ma - jo - ri - ty   the be - ne - fit   a - massed

e   -   ven   for - ward   mi - ra - cle

dou - ble   re - bel   gal - le - ry

Exercises

The central vowel *ûr* [ɜ] as in *burr*

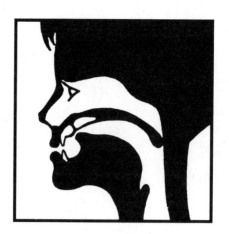

Description

For the sound of *ûr* [ɜ], a vowel is blended with the sound of the consonant [r]. [ɜ] is used only in syllables of primary or secondary stress. and is classified as a mid-central vowel.

Tongue

The tip of the tongue is retracted and raised to a central position in the mouth. The suspended tongue tip points toward the boundary of the teeth ridge and hard palate. The sides of the tongue touch the side teeth. Air passes across the center of the tongue.

Jaw

Slightly lowered.

Lips

Unrounded.

Soft Palate

Raised, closing off the nasal passageway.

The symbol ûr [ɜ] is referred to by its sound or by its name, the hooked reversed epsilon.

Common Problems

Many people are unaware that *ûr* [ɜ], as in the word *burr*, is considered a vowel sound in our language. The *ûr* [ɜ] is an r-colored vowel, produced with the tip of the tongue retracted and suspended in the center of the mouth.

In English there are two IPA symbols used to represent the *ûr* sound. The symbol *ûr* [ɜ], presented in this exercise, is used only in stressed syllables. The *hooked schwa* [ɚ], presented in the next exercise, is used only in unstressed syllables. Both symbols have a small mark on the upper part of the symbol which indicates the r-coloring of the vowel.

A. Practice the stressed *ûr* [ɝ] sound.

Read aloud these words to identify the *ûr* [ɝ].

c<u>ur</u>l   unf<u>ur</u>l   v<u>er</u>se   w<u>or</u>th   l<u>ear</u>n   s<u>ur</u>f

b<u>ir</u>th   h<u>ur</u>t   s<u>ur</u>ge   j<u>er</u>k   s<u>er</u>ve   s<u>ear</u>ch

Read aloud these sounds to contrast the *ûr* [ɝ] and *uh* [ʌ] sounds.

[ɝ]	[ʌ]	[ɝ]	[ʌ]
burst	bust	girl	gull
curb	cub	hurt	hut
dirt	done	lurk	luck

Read aloud these sounds. Feel the position of your raised tongue tip for *ûr* [ɝ].

[bɝ] [pɝ] [bɝ] [pɝ]

[ɝb] [ɝp] [ɝb] [ɝp]

B. Transcribe these words into IPA symbols.

1. irk   [ɝk]   8. her   _____
2. earn _____   9. sir   _____
3. fur   _____   10. firm   _____
4. nurse _____   11. skirt   _____
5. burst _____   12. verb   _____
6. girl   _____   13. Turk   _____
7. term _____   14. curl   _____

C. Transcribe these IPA symbols into English words.

1. [lɝk] _____   8. [wɝd] _____
2. [kɝb] _____   9. ['pɝ fɪkt] _____
3. [dɝt] _____   10. [fɝn] _____
4. [wɝl d] _____   11. ['mɝ sɪ] _____
5. [fɝ] _____   12. ['pɝ sən] _____
6. [pɝr] _____   13. ['mɝ ˌmeɪd] _____
7. ['sɝ kəl] _____   14. ['fɝ vɪd] _____

The ûr vowels are not conducive to free singing because of the tense retracted tongue. Many singers choose to replace the r-colored ûr vowels with the r-less ûr [ɜ], the sound Southerners make when they drop their r in words like herd, bird, burr, earth. *Refer to Exercise* [ɜ] *for further discussion.*

D. Transcribe these nonsense words into orthographic spellings.

1. ['sɝ vɪ] _____   3. [ˌsi 'wɝ zə] _____
2. [də 'mɝ] _____   4. ['wɝ bɪ] _____

Exercises
The central vowel *hooked schwa* [ɚ] as in *butt<u>er</u>*

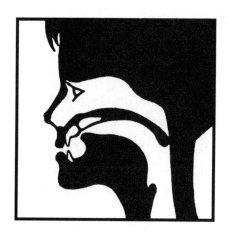

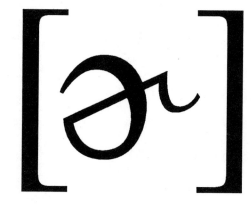

Description

Although the *unstressed ûr* [ɚ] has the same sound as the *stressed ûr* [ɝ], it is more lax and shorter in duration, and used only in unstressed syllables. It is classified as a mid-central vowel and is called *hooked schwa*.

Tongue

The tip of the tongue is retracted and raised to a central position in the mouth. The suspended tip points toward the teeth ridge and hard palate. The sides of the tongue touch the side teeth. Air passes across the center of the tongue.

Jaw

Relaxed, in a mid-high position.

Lips

Slightly open and unrounded.

Soft Palate

Raised, closing off the nasal passageway.

Common Problems

Excessive retraction, pulling the tongue too far back in the mouth and curling the tongue tip too far back toward the palate.

A. Practice the *hooked schwa* [ɚ] sound.

Read aloud these words to identify the sound of *hooked schwa* [ɚ].

giv<u>er</u> ['gɪ vɚ]	mot<u>or</u> ['moʊ tɚ]
alt<u>ar</u> ['ɔl tɚ]	act<u>or</u> ['æk tɚ]
clam<u>or</u> ['klæ mɚ]	s<u>ur</u>viv<u>or</u> [sɚ 'vaɪ vɚ]
murd<u>er</u> ['mɝ dɚ]	summ<u>er</u> ['sʌ mɚ]

The hooked schwa [ɚ] is used in English as the vowel of an unstressed syllable.

B. Transcribe the following words into IPA symbols. Use the hooked schwa [ɚ] for each unstressed r-colored vowel.

1. suffer   ['sʌ fɚ]
2. factor   _____
3. pillar   _____
4. dollar   _____
5. flavor   _____
6. labor   _____
7. scepter   _____
8. tractor   _____
9. mirror   _____
10. surfer   _____

C. Transcribe the following words, using two different IPA spellings.

In the first column use the *hooked schwa* [ɚ]. In the second column, use the *schwa* [ə] *followed* by the consonant [r]. The singer may use the pronunciation in the second column to avoid a tight tone produced by the *hooked schwa*. Read these words aloud as you transcribe them, feeling the lifted tongue tip for [ɚ] and the lowered tongue tip for [ə] and the slight lift for [r].

	[ɚ]	[ər]
1. lumber	['lʌm bɚ]	['lʌm bər]
2. rarer	_____	_____
3. permitted	_____	_____
4. better	_____	_____
5. tremor	_____	_____
6. perhaps	_____	_____

D. Transcribe these IPA symbols into English words.

1. ['skɪ pɚ] _____
2. ['pæ tɚ] _____
3. ['stɑr tɚ] _____
4. [pɚ 'fɔrm] _____
5. ['fri zɚ] _____
6. [pɚ 'sɪst] _____

E. Vocalize using *hooked schwa* [ɚ] and *schwa* [ə].

collar	[kɑ --------------- lɚ -----------]
	[kɑ --------------- lə ----------r]
effort	[ɛ --------------- fɚ -------- t]
	[ɛ --------------- fə -------rt]

Exercises

The central vowel, *r-less ûr* [ɜ] as in b<u>ir</u>d

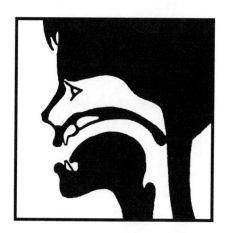

Description

The sound of the *r-less ûr* [ɜ] resembles the vowel that speakers with a Southern drawl use when they pronounce a word like *bird* [bɜd].

The *r-less ûr* [ɜ] is used only in stressed syllables. The sounds *r-less ûr* [ɜ] and *schwa* [ə] exist in a stressed-unstressed relationship comparable to *uh* [ʌ] and *schwa* [ə] as presented in previous lessons.

Tongue

The tongue is arched with the high point in a mid-central position in the mouth. The middle of the tongue is higher than for *uh* [ʌ] or *schwa* [ə]. The tip of the tongue touches the back of the bottom front teeth. The tip is not retracted for this sound.

Jaw

Dropped to a mid-low position.

Lips

Open and slightly rounded.

Soft Palate

Raised, closing off the nasal passageway.

The sound *r-less ûr* [ɜ] can be used in any word normally spoken with *r-colored ûr* [ɝ]. It is usually used by Eastern, Southern and British speakers in such words as *bird* [bɜd] or *herd* [hɜd], in which they omit the [r].

Like most vowels, [ɜ] can be referred to by its sound. Some speakers find it difficult to isolate this sound and they choose to refer to it as *r-less ûr* or *reversed epsilon*.

A. Practice the *r-less ûr* [ɜ] sound.

Read aloud these sounds. Feel the tip of the tongue touching the back of your bottom front teeth.

[bɜ] [pɜ] [bɜ] [pɜ]
[ɜb] [ɜp] [ɜb] [ɜp]

Read aloud these sounds. Feel the tip of your tongue move up and back to become suspended in the middle of the mouth for the *r-colored ûr* [ɝ].

[pɝ] [pɝ] [bɝ] [bɝ]
[ɝp] [ɝb] [ɝp] [ɝb]

Read aloud these sounds to contrast [ɝ] and [ɜ]. Feel the difference between the placement of the tongue for these two sounds and the slight lip rounding for [ɜ].

[ɝ ɜ]   [ɝ ɜ]   [ɝ ɜ]
[kɝ] [kɜ] [kɝ] [kɜ] [kɝ] [kɜ]
[zɝ] [zɜ] [zɝ] [zɜ] [zɝ] [zɜ]

Read aloud these words, using [ɜ] followed by [r].

[sɜ]	[sɜ]	[sɜ]	['sɜr vɪs]	(service)
[sɜ]	[sɜ]	[sɜ]	['sɜr lɔɪn]	(sirloin)
[wɜ]	[wɜ]	[wɜ]	[wɜrd]	(word)
[kɜ]	[kɜ]	[kɜ]	[kɜrd]	(curd)
[bɜ]	[bɜ]	[bɜ]	[bɜrst]	(burst)
[pɜ]	[pɜ]	[pɜ]	[pɜrs]	(purse)
[mɜ]	[mɜ]	[mɜ]	['mɜr təl]	(myrtle)

Read aloud these words contrasting the pronunciations of *r-colored ûr* [ɝ] and *r-less ûr* [ɜ].

	[ɝ]	[ɜ]
earn	[ɝn]	[ɜrn]
fur	[fɝ]	[fɜr]
nurse	[nɝs]	[nɜrs]
term	[tɝm]	[tɜrm]
curb	[kɝb]	[kɜrb]
skirt	[skɝt]	[skɜrt]
flirt	[flɝt]	[flɜrt]
spurn	[spɝn]	[spɜrn]

B. Transcribe the following words into IPA symbols. Use [ɜ] followed by the consonant [r] in each stressed syllable.

1. squirm [skwɜrm]   13. burr _____
2. firm [fɜrm]   14. lurk _____
3. learn [lɜrn]   15. fern _____
4. pearl _____   16. earnest _____
5. worry _____   17. hurl _____
6. curly _____   18. Berkley _____
7. curve _____   19. purr _____
8. furlough _____   20. first _____
9. curdle _____   21. hurdle _____
10. sperm _____   22. nervous _____
11. girdle _____   23. turtle _____
12. turban _____   24. turmoil _____

C. Transcribe these IPA symbols into English words.

1. [wɜrk] _____   6. ['sɜ rɪ] _____
2. [dɜrt] _____   7. ['pɜr fɪkt] _____
3. ['mɜr sɪ] _____   8. ['sɜr ˌveɪ] _____
4. ['pɜr sən] _____   9. ['pɜr mə nəns] _____
5. ['mɜr dər] _____   10. [bɜrn] _____

D. Transcribe these nonsense words into English words.

1. [sɜrs] _____   3. [zɜrk] _____
2. [ˌbɜr 'fu] _____   4. [nɜrn] _____

E. Vocalize, using [ɜ] in stressed syllables.

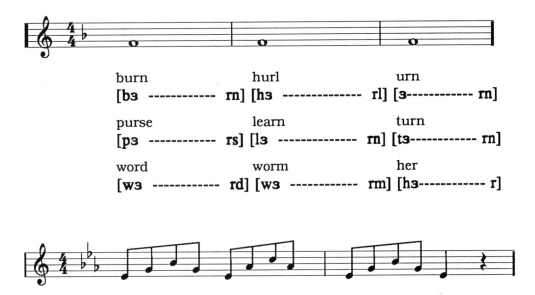

Chapter 6 Worksheet 1

Transcribe these words into IPA symbols:

1. Ernest	[ˈɝnəst]	16. alert	[əˈlɝt]
2. ultra	[ˈʌltrə]	17. lover	[ˈlʌvər]
3. upper	[ˈʌpər]	18. abrupt	[əˈbrʌpt]
4. blur	[blɝr]	19. concur	[kənˈkɝr]
5. under	[ˈʌndər]	20. blunder	[ˈblʌndər]
6. rubber	[ˈrʌbər]	21. curler	[ˈkɝlər]
7. burden	[ˈbɝdən]	22. nurse	[ˈnɝrs]
8. purse	[ˈpɝrs]	23. nerve	[ˈnɝrv]
9. lurk	[ˈlɝrk]	24. cupboard	[ˈkʌbərd]
10. fervor	[ˈfɝrvər]	25. wormwood	[ˈwɝrm‚wʊd]
11. unmask	[ənˈmæsk]	26. perk	[ˈpɝrk]
12. fundamental	[fʌndəˈmɛtəl]	27. Christmas	[ˈkrɪsməs]
13. tough	[tʌf]	28. written	[ˈrɪtən]
14. imitate	[ˈɪmə‚teɪt]	29. blood	[ˈblʌd]
15. stuff	[stʌf]	30. radium	[ˈreɪdiəm]

Transcribe these IPA symbols into English words.

1. [dʌv]	dove	6. [dɪ ˈzɝv]	deserve
2. [hɜrt]	hurt	7. [vɝb]	verb
3. [ˈleɪ bər]	labor	8. [ə ˈweɪ]	away
4. [ʌs]	us	9. [sʌm]	some
5. [ˈvɪk tər]	victor	10. [wɝr]	were

Chapter 6 Worksheet 2

Transcribe these words into IPA symbols:

1. heard   [hɜrd]
2. perhaps   [pər'hæps]
3. surplus   ['sɜrpləs]
4. surfboard   ['sɜrfbɔrd]
5. lucky   ['lʌki]

6. serpent   ['sɜrpənt]
7. nursery   ['nɜrsəri]
8. river   [rɪvər]
9. deliver   [dɪ'lɪvər]
10. trouble   [trʌbəl]

11. fur   [fɜr]
12. cup   [kʌp]
13. once   [wʌns]
14. dug   [dʌg]
15. plunder   ['plʌndər]

16. honey   ['hʌni]
17. ballast   ['bæləst]
18. vigorous   ['vɪgərəs]
19. butter   [bʌtər]
20. purr   [pɜr]

21. money   [mʌni]
22. putt   [pʌt]
23. visitor   ['vɪzətər]
24. flippant   ['flɪpənt]
25. stir   [stɜr]

26. enough   [ɪ'nʌf]
27. furnace   ['fɜrnəs]
28. person   ['pɜrsən]
29. worker   ['wɜrkər]
30. girl   [gɜrl]

Transcribe these IPA symbols into English words.

1. ['peɪ pər]   paper
2. ['mɜr mər]   murmur
3. ['dʌ bəl]   double
4. [krʌst]   crust
5. [sɜr]   sir
6. [wɜrm]   worm
7. [fɜrst]   first
8. [plʌmp]   plump
9. ['par lər]   parlor
10. ['kʌ dəl]   cuddle

CHAPTER 7
DIPHTHONGS

Introduction to Diphthongs

A diphthong, pronounced [ˈdɪf θɔŋ] occurs when two vowels in the same syllable are blended together to form a single vowel unit.

Two vowels existing next to each other in a word do not necessarily produce a diphthong. For example, in the word *chaotic* [ke ˈɑ tɪk] the vowels *a* and *o* are next to each other, but in two different syllables. They are heard as two distinct vowel units and do not become a diphthong.

Sometimes when two vowel letters are next to each other in the same syllable, as the *au* in *audit* [ˈɔ dɪt], the result is a single pure vowel sound, not a diphthong.

A pure vowel is one which is produced without movement of the articulators. By contrast, a diphthong is produced when there is a movement of the tongue, lips or jaw during the production of a vowel, usually with a quick, gliding motion of the tongue to a higher position. The two vowel sounds of a diphthong are blended into a sound which the speaker perceives as a single unit. There are six diphthongs in English, four are phonemes and two are allophones.

The phoneme [aɪ] as in *high*, composed of the pure vowel [a] and the glide [ɪ].

The phoneme [aʊ] as in *house*, composed of the pure vowel [a] and the glide [ʊ].

The phoneme [ɔɪ] as in *boy*, composed of the pure vowel [ɔ] and the glide [ɪ].

The phoneme [ju] as in *use* [juz], composed of the glide [j], as in *yes*, and the pure vowel [u].

The allophone [eɪ] as in *bait*, composed of the pure [e] and the glide [ɪ].

The allophone [oʊ] as in *boat*, composed of the pure [o] and the glide [ʊ].

The diphthongs [eɪ] and [oʊ], which were presented in Chapters 4 and 5, have a different character from the remaining four diphthongs. For instance, whether the speaker pronounces a word with a diphthongal [eɪ] or a pure [e] (omitting the glide), the meaning of the word remains the same. *Baby* ['beɪ bɪ] and *baby* ['be bɪ] would be both perceived as a word referring to a small child. The same is true of words which use the vowel [oʊ]. Whether the word *hope* is pronounced as [hoʊp] or [hop], it would indicate the same meaning. The lack of change in meaning of the words makes the diphthongal [eɪ] and [oʊ] allophones of the phonemes [e] and [o].

However, if the speaker omits the glides from the diphthongs [aɪ], [aʊ], [ɔɪ] or [ju], and says only the stronger vowel, the meaning of the word changes. Read aloud these words.

Height [haɪt] becomes *hot* [hat].

House [haʊs] becomes *hass* [has].

Joy [jɔɪ] becomes *jaw* [jɔ].

Abuse [ə 'bjus] becomes *a booze* [ə 'buz].

These four diphthongs, [aɪ], [aʊ], [ɔɪ] and [ju], are thus shown to be separate, distinct phonemes. In true diphthongs, even though two symbols are used, the symbols are representative of one phoneme, and both vowel sounds are needed to maintain the meaning of the word.

Exercises

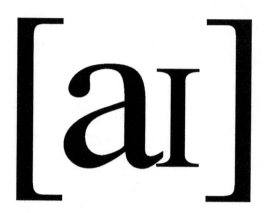

The diphthong [aɪ] **as in** *h<u>igh</u>*

Description

Tongue

The tongue begins in a low position for *bright ah* [a], then quickly glides to a high, forward position for *ih* [ɪ]. Only the blade and middle part of the tongue move upward to create the glide [ɪ]. The tip of the tongue remains behind the back of the bottom teeth.

Jaw

The jaw drops to a low position for *bright ah* [a], and closes slightly for *ih* [ɪ]. In singing, the tongue is usually used to accomplish the glide [ɪ].

Lips

Open and unrounded.

Soft Palate

Raised, closing off the nasal passageway.

Common Problems

The substitution of pure [a] for the diphthong [aɪ], usually in Southern dialect. Saying *I'm* as [am] instead of [aɪm].

The substitution of [ə] for the glide [ɪ], caused by not raising the tongue to a high, forward position for [ɪ]. Saying *tight* as [taət] instead of [taɪt].

The substitution of a sound similar to the *short o* [ɒ] or *aw* [ɔ] in the diphthong [aɪ], caused by pulling the tongue too far back and by rounding the lips slightly. An example would be asking: "*Were you hard-back?*" instead of "*Were you hired back?*"

To become more familiar with the articulation of the diphthong [aɪ], sustain the sound *bah.....*, then glide from that sound toward the vowel *ee* [i] as in the word *eat. Bah.....eat.* Notice the movement of your tongue as you move from *bah* to *eat.*

Then read aloud the word *buy* [baɪ] and notice the similar movement of your tongue as you pronounce the diphthong [aɪ]. On the glide of [ɪ], the tongue does not move as high as [i], so we transcribe it as the laxer [ɪ].

A. Practice the diphthong [aɪ].

Read aloud these sounds.

[baɪ] [paɪ]   [baɪ] [paɪ]
[aɪb] [aɪp]   [aɪb] [aɪp]

Read aloud these words to identify **[aɪ]**.

style	aisle
silent	Cairo
child	why
choirs	heighten
item	thigh
flying	beguile
pies	Mike
buy	spy
island	geyser

Read aloud these words to contrast the diphthong **[aɪ]** and pure **[a]**.

[aɪ]	[a]
hi	ha
right	rot
eye's	ahs
by	bah
slights	slots
height	hot

B. Transcribe these words into IPA symbols.

1. tried [traɪd]
2. ride _____
3. I _____
4. high _____
5. ideas _____
6. fine _____
7. ice _____

8. rhyme _____
9. deny _____
10. Clyde _____
11. hides _____
12. spider _____
13. try _____
14. light _____

C. Transcribe these IPA symbols into English words.

1. [dɪ 'skraɪb] _____
2. [taɪm] _____
3. [naɪt] _____
4. [taɪd] _____
5. [praɪz]_____
6. ['ɛr ˌlaɪn] _____
7. ['fraɪ dɪ] _____

8. [braɪdz]_____
9. ['traɪ bəl] _____
10. [smaɪl] _____
11. [maɪt] _____
12. ['aɪ dəl] _____
13. [kraɪ] _____
14. [gaɪd] _____

D. Transcribe these nonsense words into orthographic spellings.

1. ['zaɪ gəm] _____
2. ['gaɪ wɑ]_____

3.['grɛ laɪ] _____
4.[də 'taɪ]_____

E. Vocalize, articulating each [aɪ] clearly and easily. When
singing, sustain the first part of the diphthong [a], and then
glide to [ɪ] just as you release the note.

high
[ha————————————————ɪ]
pie
[pa————————————————ɪ]

lots _____ lights
ha _____ hi
rot _____ right

tired   mind   line
fly   buy   lie

kite   light   climb   fine
my   why   wine   flight
prize   slide   twice   size

The diphthong [aʊ] as in *hou**se***

Exercises

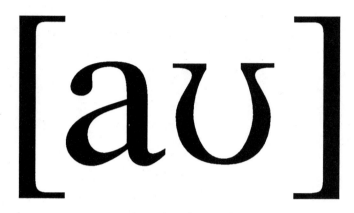

Description

Tongue

The tongue begins in a low position for *bright ah* [a], then quickly glides to a high, back position for *ŏŏ* [ʊ]. Only the back of the tongue moves to create the glide [ʊ]. The tip of the tongue remains behind the back of the bottom front teeth.

Jaw

The jaw is dropped to a low position.

Lips

The lips are open and unrounded for [a], then move to a rounded position for [ʊ].

Soft Palate

Raised, closing off the nasal passageway.

Common Problems

The substitution of pure [a] for the diphthong [aʊ], usually in Southern dialect.

The substitution of [æ] for [a], caused by bringing the tongue too high and forward for [aʊ].

The substitution of [ə] for [ʊ], caused by not rounding the lips for [ʊ].

Nasalizing [aʊ] by speaking through the nose. This most often occurs before *m, n,* and *ng,* but is also found in other positions.

To become more familiar with the articulation of the diphthong [aʊ], sustain the sound *ha......*, then glide from the sound toward the word *ooze*. Notice the movements of your lips and tongue as you move from *ha* to *ooze*. Then read aloud the word *house* [haʊs] and notice the similar movements of your lips and tongue as you pronounce the diphthong [aʊ].

A. Practice the diphthong [aʊ] as in *house*.

Read aloud these sounds.

[baʊ] [paʊ] [baʊ] [paʊ]

[aʊp] [aʊb] [aʊp] [aʊb]

Read aloud these words to identity [aʊ].

b<u>ou</u>nd	<u>ou</u>t
tr<u>ou</u>t	c<u>ow</u>
t<u>o</u>wel	br<u>ow</u>
sa<u>ue</u>rkr<u>au</u>t	al<u>ou</u>d
pl<u>ou</u>gh	h<u>ou</u>r

Read aloud these words to contrast [æ] and [aʊ].

[æ]	[aʊ]
catch	couch
hand	hound
mass	mouse
pat	pout
sand	sound

To avoid producing the flat, raised sound of [æ] in the diphthong [aʊ], be sure to drop your jaw and give [a] its full open space.

Read aloud these words, contrasting pure [a] and diphthongal [aʊ].

[a]	[aʊ]
ha	how
pot	pout
fond	found
bra	brow
clot	clout

Be sure to round your lips for the ŏŏ [ʊ] glide. Do not eliminate the glide [ʊ] nor substitute the unrounded schwa [ə].

Read aloud these words, being careful not to nasalize the [aʊ].

> brown
>
> down
>
> found
>
> town
>
> lounge
>
> fountain
>
> noun

B. Transcribe these words into IPA symbols.

1. gown [gaʊn]
2. rowdy _____
3. allow _____
4. announce _____
5. prowler _____
6. pout _____
7. ounces _____
8. found _____
9. plow _____
10. brown _____
11. frown _____
12. mountain _____
13. ours _____
14. boundary _____

C. Transcribe these IPA symbols into English words.

1. [raʊnd] _____
2. [braʊ] _____
3. [plaʊd] _____
4. [saʊnd] _____
5. [traʊt] _____
6. [praʊd] _____
7. [kaʊ] _____
8. [vaʊd] _____
9. [raʊ] _____
10. [maʊnd] _____

D. Transcribe these nonsense words into IPA symbols.

1. [braʊk] _____
2. ['taʊ ˌkɛt] _____
3. [daʊg] _____
4. ['vaʊ kən] _____

E. Vocalize, articulating each [aʊ] carefully and easily. When singing, sustain the first part of the diphthong [a], gliding to [ʊ] just as you release the note.

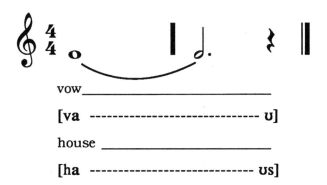

vow_____

[va --------------------------- ʊ]

house _____

[ha --------------------------- ʊs]

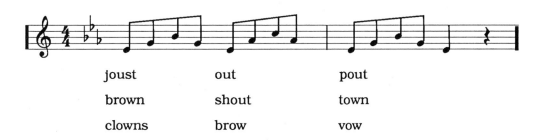

joust	out	pout
brown	shout	town
clowns	brow	vow

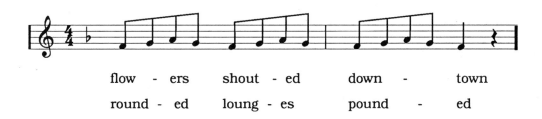

flow - ers	shout - ed	down - town
round - ed	loung - es	pound - ed

Exercises

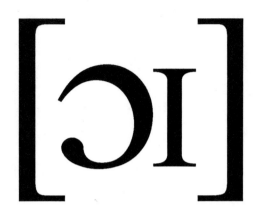

Description

Tongue

The tongue begins in a low, back position for *aw* [ɔ], then quickly glides to a high, forward position for *ih* [ɪ]. The tip of the tongue remains behind the back of the bottom front teeth.

Jaw

Dropped to a low position.

Lips

Rounded for [ɔ], then relaxed for the glide [ɪ].

Soft Palate

Raised, closing off the nasal passageway.

Common Problems

The substitution of pure [ɔ] for diphthong [ɔɪ], omitting the glide [ɪ].

To substitution of [ə] for the glide [ɪ]. In addition, some speakers add the [w] or *y* [j], so that a word such as *toil* sounds like [tɔwəl].

The substitution of the diphthong [aɪ] for [ɔɪ] occurs occasionally in North American speech. The lips do not round and the jaw is not sufficiently dropped when beginning the diphthong. *Toil* [tɔɪl] sounds like *tile* [taɪl].

To become more familiar with the articulation of the diphthong [ɔɪ], sustain the sound *caw......*, then glide from that sound toward the word *eat*. Feel the movements of your lips and tongue as you move from *caw* to *eat*. Then read aloud the word *coil* [kɔɪl] and notice the similar movements of your lips and tongue as you pronounce the diphthong [ɔɪ].

A. Practice the diphthong *oy* [ɔɪ] as in boy.

Read aloud these sounds.

[bɔɪ] [pɔɪ] [bɔɪ] [pɔɪ]

[ɔɪb] [ɔɪp] [ɔɪb] [ɔɪp]

Read aloud these words containing the diphthong [ɔɪ].

<u>oy</u>ster

b<u>oi</u>l

c<u>oy</u>

j<u>oi</u>n

depl<u>oy</u>

destr<u>oy</u>

Read aloud these words to avoid the use of [w] or the replacement of the glide *ih* [ɪ] with *schwa* [ə].

[ɔɪ]	[ɔə]	[ɔw]
poise	not paws	nor paw was
joys	not jaws	nor jaw was
noise	not gnaws	nor gnaw was

Read aloud these words, and be careful not to omit the glide *ih* [ɪ] nor replace it with a *schwa* [ə].

[ɔ]	diphthong [ɔɪ]
all	oil
Saul	soil
tall	toil
ball	boil
fall	foil
call	coil

IPA for Singers

B. Transcribe these words into IPA symbols.

1. coin [kɔɪn]   8. toy _____
2. ointment _____ 9. broil _____
3. Hoyle _____   10. oyster _____
4. royal _____   11. turmoil _____
5. soil _____   12. avoid _____
6. oily _____   13. recoil _____
7. foibles _____ 14. exploited _____

C. Transcribe these IPA symbols into English words.

1. [fɔɪl] _____   6. [kɔɪ] _____
2. [pɔɪz] _____   7. [spɔɪl] _____
3. [sɔɪld] _____ 8. [tɔɪz] _____
4. [ə 'nɔɪd] _____ 9. [ə 'drɔɪt] _____
5. [hɔɪst] _____ 10. [tɔɪld] _____

D. Transcribe these nonsense words into English words.

1. [lɔɪt] _____   3. ['kɔɪ zəm]_____
2. [ˌni 'fɔɪ] _____ 4. [sɔɪz] _____

120

E. Vocalize and articulate each *oy* [ɔɪ] clearly and easily.

When singing a diphthong [ɔɪ], be sure to sustain the [ɔ],
and add the glide [ɪ] only as you release the note.

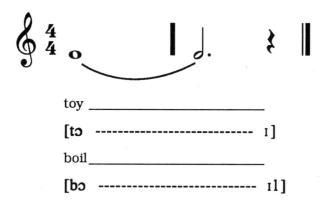

toy _____

[tɔ --------------------------- ɪ]

boil_____

[bɔ --------------------------- ɪl]

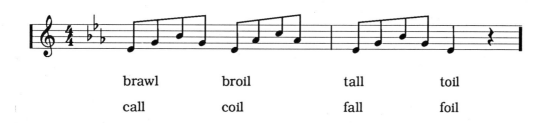

| brawl | broil | tall | toil |
| call | coil | fall | foil |

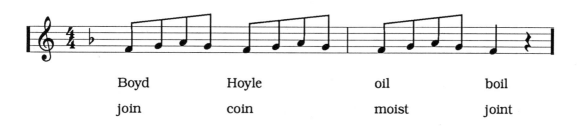

| Boyd | Hoyle | oil | boil |
| join | coin | moist | joint |

Exercises

The diphthong [ju] as in *ab<u>u</u>se*

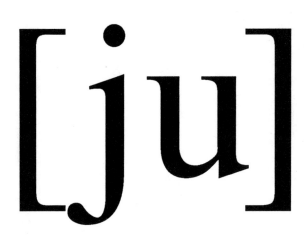

Description

The first part of the diphthong [ju] is formed by the gliding sound of *y* as in *yes*. The *y* sound is represented by the IPA symbol [j] , which is named *yot* [jɔt].

Tongue

The tongue begins in a high, forward position for the sound of *yot* [j], then quickly moves to a high, back position for o͞o [u]. The tip of the tongue remains behind the back of the bottom front teeth.

Jaw

Relaxed.

Lips

Unrounded for *yot* [j], then immediately rounding to produce o͞o [u].

Soft Palate

Raised, closing off the nasal passageway.

Common Problems

*The glide **yot** [jɔt] will be fully discussed in Chapter 13, Glides.*

The use of the diphthong [ju] is in transition in American speech. Following a [d], [n] or [t], either [ju] or [u] is now considered standard. Many speakers, however, prefer to maintain [ju] in these words, saying *dew* [dju] instead of *do* [du].

The diphthong [ju], as in *abuse*, differs from the other three diphthongs in this chapter in that the glide portion occurs at the beginning instead of the end of the diphthong. To produce the [ju] diphthong, you will begin with your tongue in a high, forward position like *ih* [ɪ]. The tongue moves quickly from that position, not remaining there long enough to produce the full vowel sound of [ɪ]. The gliding movement produces the sound of *yot* [jɔt]. It will be fully discussed in Chapter 13, Glides.

Your tongue will quickly glide back from the forward position of *yot* [j] to the high, back position of the vowel *oo* [u]. You can feel this movement dramatically if you will lightly touch the front of your tongue with your forefinger as you say the diphthong [ju]. The forward tongue of [j] will snap back quickly for [u]. You can feel the sudden movement of the tongue as it leaves your finger.

A. Practicing the diphthong [ju].

Read aloud these words with initial [ju].

use	eulogy
unit	uniform
usual	euphony

Read aloud these words with medial [ju].

abuse	refuse
amuse	viewer
cube	puberty
fewer	mutilated
music	bureau
huge	curious

Read aloud these words. Use either [ju] or [u] according to your preference. Consistency is desirable but not mandatory.

Following a [d], [n], or [t] both the diphthong [ju] and the pure vowel [u] are considered standard.

due	tube
dew	tulip
exude	Tuesday
new	numeral
nude	nuclear

Read aloud these words. Contemporary General American speech shows a preference for the pure vowel [u] when preceded by the sounds [s], [z], [l] or th [θ].

suit	suitor
lute	Lutheran
resume	absolutely
suitcase	enthusiasm

B. Transcribe these words into IPA symbols. Each word contains the diphthong [ju].

In the word cumulate **['kju mjə ˌleɪt]**, *notice that the second syllable is unstressed. The diphthong* **[ju]** *will be weakened to* **[jə]**.

1. useful ['jus fəl]
2. feudal _____
3. fume _____
4. mule _____
5. cue _____
6. mute _____
7. musical _____

8. ewe _____
9. humorous _____
10. beauty _____
11. cute _____
12. you _____
13. abuses _____
14. cumulate _____

C. Transcribe these IPA symbols into English words.

1. [pər 'fjum]_____
2. ['fju təl] _____
3. ['pju pəl] _____
4. ['pju nɪ]_____
5. ['dju əl] _____
6. [fjuz] _____
7. [ə 'kjuz] _____

8. ['jun jən] _____
9. ['ju nɪ ˌfaɪ]_____
10. [kju] _____
11. [pju] _____
12. ['ju nɪ ˌfɔrm]_____
13. [mju] _____
14. [mjul] _____

D. Transcribe these nonsense words into orthographic spellings.

1. ['zju ˌmi]_____
2. ['ju ˌkɛ ˌsɛ] _____

3. ['jum ˌdju]_____
4. [ˌbɑ 'kju təm] __

E. Vocalize on the diphthong [ju]. Glide quickly from *yot* **[j] to
the second part of the diphthong, [u].**

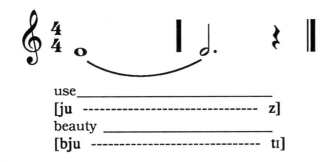

use_____

[ju --------------------------------- z]

beauty _____

[bju --------------------------- tɪ]

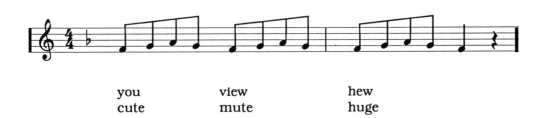

you   view   hew

cute   mute   huge

a - buse   u - nite   eu - lo - gy

Chapter 7 Worksheet 1

Transcribe these words into IPA symbols.

1. cried _____   16. mile _____

2. flounder _____   17. fuse _____

3. pie _____   18. cider _____

4. broiled _____   19. drive _____

5. gown _____   20. fly _____

6. bureau _____   21. eye _____

7. twice _____   22. beauty _____

8. pride _____   23. rice _____

9. cowboy _____   24. destroy _____

10. bike _____   25. amount _____

11. sirloin _____   26. voice _____

12. music _____   27. tower _____

13. somehow _____   28. toy _____

14. hardboiled _____   29. pure _____

15. abuse _____   30. highbrow _____

Transcribe these IPA symbols into English words.

1. [ə ˈdrɔɪt] _____   6. [kə ˈraʊz] _____

2. [skaʊt] _____   7. [ˈdi ˌkɔɪ] _____

3. [blaɪt] _____   8. [ˈɑr ˌgju] _____

4. [grɔɪn] _____   9. [klaɪm] _____

5. [ju ˈnaɪt] _____   10. [klaʊd] _____

Chapter 7 Worksheet 2

Transcribe these words into IPA symbols.

1. avoid _____
2. pointed _____
3. doily _____
4. ploy _____
5. hike _____

6. ground _____
7. rites _____
8. Bible _____
9. pupil _____
10. cue _____

11. convoy _____
12. trout _____
13. cloister _____
14. employ _____
15. beautiful _____

16. moist _____
17. proud _____
18. cloud _____
19. unity _____
20. soy _____

21. oysters _____
22. utility _____
23. hour _____
24. tribal _____
25. loud _____

26. crowded _____
27. kite _____
28. proudly _____
29. accused _____
30. poise _____

Transcribe these IPA symbols into English words.

1. ['daɪ ət] _____
2. [skaɪ] _____
3. [spraɪt] _____
4. [rɪ 'naʊnd] _____
5. [flaɪt] _____

6. [saʊr] _____
7. [aɪ 'diəl] _____
8. [prə 'vaɪd] _____
9. [ju nə 'vɜr səl] _____
10. [ɪn 'saɪt fəl] _____

CHAPTER 8
CONSONANTS

Introduction to Consonants

Now that you are familiar with the IPA symbols for vowels, you will find it easy to learn the remaining symbols for the consonants of English. Of the twenty-five symbols for consonants in the International Phonetic Alphabet, sixteen are identical to the letters in the English alphabet. That leaves only nine new symbols to be learned. Figure 12 shows the IPA symbols used for English consonants.

Classification of Consonants

A *consonant* is a speech sound that is formed when the articulators interrupt the flow of air through the vocal tract. The *place* of articulation, the *manner* of articulation, and *voicing* of a consonant determine its classification.

The *place* of articulation refers to the place in the vocal tract where the interruption of the air flow occurs. For example, the *place* of articulation for the consonant [p] is at the lips, because the flow of breath is interrupted at the lips. The points of the vocal tract where breath interruption occurs to produce consonants are: the *lips, teeth, tongue, teeth ridge, hard palate, soft palate* and *glottis*. See the drawing of the vocal tract in Figure 8, page 13 (Oral Cavity and Its Articulators).

Figure 12: The IPA Symbols for English Consonants

	IPA Symbol	Sound	English word
Stop plosives	[p]	p	pet
	[b]	b	bet
	[t]	t	toe
	[d]	d	doe
	[k]	k	kit
	[g]	g	give
Nasals	[m]	m	moon
	[n]	n	neat
→	[ŋ]	ng	hung
Fricatives	[f]	f	feet
	[v]	v	vain
→	[θ]	unvoiced th	think
→	[ð]	voiced th	than
	[s]	s	sea
	[z]	z	zip
→	[ʃ]	unvoiced sh	she
→	[ʒ]	voiced zh	azure
	[h]	h	heat
Lateral	[l]	l	lift
Glides	[r]	r	rose
	[j]	y	yes
	[hw]	unvoiced w	when
	[w]	voiced w	were
Combination Consonants	[tʃ]	unvoiced ch	cheek
→	[dʒ]	voiced j	jeer, gin

The *manner* of articulation refers to the method of interruption of the breath flow, whether by a complete interruption or by a partial interruption in the flow of air. In the production of the [p] consonant, for example, the air flow is completely stopped before being released suddenly. The various manners of articulation include:

1. *Stop-plosive* — the air flow is completely prevented from passing through the mouth or the nose and then is released suddenly. Examples: [p b k g].

2. *Fricative* — the air flow is partially interrupted, thus producing a noisy sound. Examples: [f v s z].

3. *Nasal* — the vocal tract is blocked at some point within the oral cavity, but the dropped soft palate allows air to travel through the nasal passageway. There are only three nasal consonants in English: [m n] and *ng* [ŋ].

4. *Lateral* — the tongue tip lifts to touch the teeth and the teeth ridge and the breath flows past one or both sides of the tongue. The [l] consonant is the only lateral consonant in English.

5. *Glide* — the sound is characterized by a movement of the articulators from one position to another. Examples: [r], [j] as in *yes* and [w] as in *wind*.

6. *Combination Consonants* — the sound is produced by a stop-plosive followed by a fricative consonant, forming a single sound. The two combination consonants in English, [ʧ] as in *cheek* and [ʤ] as in *jeer*, are sometimes called affricatives.

The classification of *voicing* indicates whether the consonant is produced with vocal fold vibration (*voiced*) or without vocal fold vibration (*unvoiced*). To determine whether a consonant is voiced, simply place your hand on your throat and speak the consonant. If you feel vibration, the consonant is voiced and has pitch. In English, there are several pairs of consonants (called cognates) which have the same place and manner of articulation. Cognates are differentiated only by the voicing.

Example:	Unvoiced	Voiced
	[p]	[b]
	[s]	[z]
	[t]	[d]
	[k]	[g]
	[f]	[v]

The following chart represents the classification of consonants according to the place and manner of articulation and voicing. Any unfamiliar symbols will be pointed out as they occur in forthcoming exercises.

Figure 13: The Classification of Consonants

	Place of Articulation													
	Both Lips		Upper Teeth and Lower Lips		Tongue and Upper Teeth		Tongue and Teeth Ridge		Tongue and Hard Palate		Tongue and Soft Palate		Glottis	
	unv.	v.	unv.	v.	unv.	v.	unv.	v.	unv.	v.	unv.	v.	unv.	v.
Fricative			f	v	θ	ð	s	z	ʃ	ʒ			h	
Stop-Plosive	p	b					t	d			k	g		
Nasal		m						n				ŋ		
Lateral										l				
Glide	hw	w								r j				

(left vertical label: **Manner of Articulation**)

Common Problems in Articulation

The most common problems in articulation are *muffledness, over-articulation, mis-articulation, substitution, addition,* and *omission* of specific consonants.

The category of *muffledness* refers to the lazy or slow use of the lips and tongue which results in indistinct, mushy articulation. Unlike vowels which have the potential for loud volume, consonants are very limited in carrying power and must be articulated with precision and clarity for words to be easily understood.

Over-articulation is exaggerated articulation which is the result of inappropriate emphasis, the separation of syllables, or excessive movement of the lips and tongue. Over-articulation is often called mouthing the words.

Mis-articulation is the distortion of one or more specific consonants. This occurs most often with *th, s, z, t, d, l* or *r*. Lisps would fall into this category of mis-articulation.

Another articulation distortion which frequently occurs is called *substitution*. The speaker or singer substitutes one consonant for another. An example would be saying *cidy* for *city*.

Some speakers make *additions* of inappropriate sounds in some words, such as saying *idear* for *idea*.

Other speakers articulate in such a way that there are *omissions* of necessary sounds. Omissions are most likely to occur in consonant clusters. An example would be to omit the *t* in *exact* or *exactly*.

The exercises which follow are designed to identify the IPA symbol for each specific consonant and to clarify the articulation of each sound. The consonants will be presented in groups according to their manner of articulation. Chapter 9 includes the stop-plosive consonants.

CHAPTER 9
THE
STOP-PLOSIVE
CONSONANTS

A stop-plosive consonant is one in which the air flow is completely stopped from passing through the mouth or nose and is then suddenly released. Stop-plosive consonants are further defined by whether the consonant is voiced (produced with vocal fold vibration) or unvoiced (without vocal fold vibration).

Cognates are paired consonants which have the same manner and place of articulation but are differentiated only because one is unvoiced and the other is voiced. Stop-plosive consonants can be grouped into three cognates. In this chapter the stop-plosive consonants will be presented in the following order:

1. The cognates [p] as in *pet* and [b] as in *bet.*

2. The cognates [t] as in *ten* and [d] as in *den.*

3. The cognates [k] as in *kit* and [g] as in *give.*

[p] [b] [t] [d] [k] [g]

Exercises

The stop-plosive consonants [p] and [b]

Description

IPA Symbol	**[p]**	**[b]**
Word Example	*pat*	*bat*
Voicing	unvoiced	voiced
Place of Articulation	both lips	
Manner of Articulation	stop-plosive The lips close. The soft palate is raised, closing the nasal passageway. Air pressure builds behind the lips and is then released plosively.	

Common problems

The substitution of unvoiced [p] for voiced [b] or the reverse. *Dabble* should not sound like *dapple.*

The omission of [p] and [b]. This error occurs most often in the medial or final position as in *clasp* or *bulb.*

Excessive vocal effort caused by building up too much breath pressure before releasing the sound.

In the exercises, keep your lips soft and relaxed as you articulate the [p] and [b] consonants. Do not tighten the lips into a straight line. Do not try to make stop-plosive consonants louder by building additional force before the plosive part of articulation. The [p] and [b] consonants are best produced when the lips, cheeks, and jaw remain loose and flexible.

When an IPA symbol is the same as the letter of the alphabet, it can be referred to by the name of the letter. For instance, [p] could be called [pi]. However, in the IPA we are dealing with sounds, not names. In the following exercise, you will read aloud the *sound* of the consonant. To pronounce the stop-plosive consonant [p], the lips will close creating a stoppage of air, then the lips open and air is released plosively. As you release the plosive part, you will hear a sound like a whispered *uh* (*schwa* [ə]). So [p] will sound like whispered *puh*. A similar sound occurs with [b]. You will hear voiced *buh*.

A. Articulation drills for [p] and [b].

The objective in this exercise is to distinguish between the unvoiced [p] and the voiced [b]. Place a finger on the front of your throat, on your Adam's apple, as you read aloud the consonants in a normal conversational loudness. Feel the vibration that occurs for [b] but not for [p].

Read aloud these sounds.

[p]	[b]
[p p]	[b b]
[p p p]	[b b b]

When more than one consonant is printed within brackets with a space between the consonants, repeat the sound.

Read aloud these paired words to contrast the sounds of [p] and [b] in these words.

pear	bear
pit	bit
pate	bait
putt	butt
ape	Abe
cap	cab
maple	Mabel
happy	abbey

Read aloud to feel the contrast between pressured and non-pressured articulation.

As you read the following words, articulate [p] and [b] forcefully (as if you were angry). Allow the breath pressure to build up excessively for the plosive part of the articulation. Feel the undesirable tension this creates in the neck and lips on [p] and [b].

poke	pun
pearly	pick
bad	burn
boy	bum

Read the words aloud a second time, articulating the [p] and [b] consonants gently. Speak the sounds clearly and without excessive pressure.

poke	pun
pearly	pick
bad	burn
boy	bum

Sing this musical pattern using a lip trill.

Put your lips together gently and blow air through them. This will result in a fluttering of the relaxed lips, the sound we make when saying, "Brrr, it is cold!" This exercise, called a lip trill, is excellent for loosening the lips and improving the consistency of breath flow.

b r r r r r r r r r r r r r r r r

B. Transcribe these words with [p] and [b] into IPA symbols.

Read aloud the words as you write them, clearly articulating each [p] and [b] in the initial, medial and final positions.

Initial

1. peg	[pɛg]	6. been	_____
2. beg	[bɛg]	7. best	_____
3. pole	_____	8. pest	_____
4. bowl	_____	9. beast	_____
5. pen	_____	10. peace	_____

Medial

1. happy	_____	6. trouble	_____
2. abbey	_____	7. rumble	_____
3. puppy	_____	8. rumple	_____
4. baby	_____	9. capable	_____
5. helpful	_____	10. probably	_____

Final

1. rip	_____	6. mob	_____
2. rib	_____	7. sop	_____
3. cap	_____	8. sob	_____
4. cab	_____	9. rope	_____
5. mop	_____	10. robe	_____

136

C. Transcribe these IPA symbols into English words.

1. ['sɪm pəl] _simple_
2. ['sɪm bəl] _symbol_
3. ['ɛm bər] _ember_
4. ['skæm pər] _scamper_
5. ['nʌm bər] _number_
6. ['pæm pər] _pamper_
7. [mæpt] _mapped_
8. ['sʌb sə ˌdaɪz] _____
9. ['ɑp tɪ məm] _____
10. [græb] _____

D. Vocalize, articulating each [p] and [b] clearly.

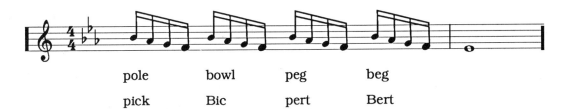

| pole | bowl | peg | beg |
| pick | Bic | pert | Bert |

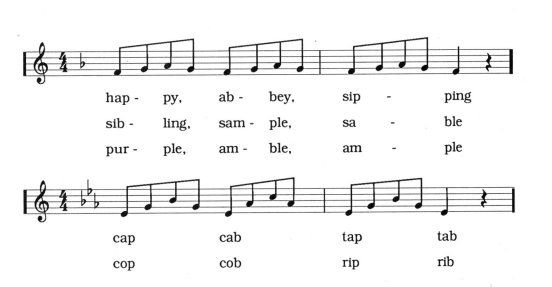

hap -	py,	ab -	bey,	sip -	ping
sib -	ling,	sam -	ple,	sa -	ble
pur -	ple,	am -	ble,	am -	ple

| cap | cab | tap | tab |
| cop | cob | rip | rib |

E. Sentences with [p] and [b].

Read aloud these sentences, articulating quickly, easily and flexibly.

Perky Patty picks pretty, pink posies.

Paul paints preposterous purple palaces.

Bouncing baby boys bring bountiful blessings.

Brett burned Brian's buttered breakfast biscuits.

Exercises

The stop-plosive consonants [t] and [d]

Description

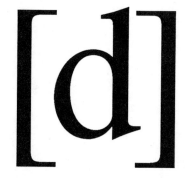

IPA Symbol	[t]	[d]
Word Example	*team*	*deem*
Voicing	unvoiced	voiced
Place of Articulation	tongue tip and teeth ridge	
Manner of Articulation	stop-plosive The tongue tip touches the teeth ridge to stop the air flow through the oral passageway. The soft palate is raised, closing the nasal passageway. Air pressure builds up and then is released explosively.	

Common problems

The substitution of unvoiced [t] for voiced [d] or the reverse. *Pretty* must not be *preddy.*

Incomplete closure causing muffledness.

The omission of [t] and [d] which occurs most often in the medial or final position as in *last* or *bland.*

Pressured articulation, building up too much pressure on the stop part of the stop-plosives [t] and [d].

A. Articulation drills for [t] and [d].

Articulate the [t] and [d] consonants by using a flexible upward movement of the tongue tip to touch the teeth ridge. Be sure to keep your jaw relaxed.

Read aloud these sounds.

Practice the following sounds in isolation to contrast the voiced and unvoiced qualities of each. Place your hand on the front of your throat, on the Adam's apple, and say the sounds [t] and [d]. Feel the vibration that occurs for [d] but not for [t].

[t]	[d]
[t t t]	[d d d]
[t t t t]	[d d d d]

Read aloud these words. Feel the contrast between pressured and non-pressured articulation.

Articulate these words forcefully (as if you were angry). Allow the breath pressure to build up excessively for the plosive part of the articulation. Feel the undesirable tension this creates in throat and neck on [t] and [d].

tie	tan
ton	toe
die	Dan
done	dough

Read these words aloud a second time, but this time gently. Articulate clearly and *without* excessive pressure or explosiveness.

tie	tan
ton	toe
die	Dan
done	dough

Read aloud these paired words to contrast the sounds of [t] and [d].

[t]	[d]
wrote	road
tight	tide
bet	bed
plotting	plodding
matter	madder
otter	odder
hoped	homed
slapped	slammed
clipped	climbed
latter	ladder
letter	(not ledder)
pretty	(not preddy)
little	(not liddle)

Notice that the final *d* is sometimes pronounced [d] and sometimes [t]. When the final *d* follows a voiced consonant sound, the *d* is pronounced as voiced [d].

> hummed [hʌmd] The *d* follows the sound of voiced [m].
> beloved [bɪ ˈlʌvd] The *d* follows the sound of voiced [v].

However, when *d* follows an unvoiced consonant sound, it is pronounced as unvoiced [t].

> clipped [klɪpt] The *d* follows the sound of unvoiced [p].
> kicked [kɪkt]. The *d* follows the sound of unvoiced [k].

Read aloud to contrast [t] with [ts].

fact	facts
pest	pests
lift	lifts
insist	insists

Read aloud to contrast [d] and [dz].

band	bands
find	finds
end	ends
friend	friends

B. Transcribe these words into IPA symbols.

Read aloud the words as you write, clearly articulating each [t] and [d] in the initial, medial and final positions.

Initial

1. toil	_____	5. din	_____
2. don	_____	6. tie	_____
3. die	_____	7. tone	_____
4. tin	_____	8. dune	_____

Medial

1. middle	_____	5. better	_____
2. attain	_____	6. lantern	_____
3. mid-day	_____	7. notice	_____
4. sounded	_____	8. mandate	[ˈmæn deɪt]

Final

1. send	_____	5. nod	_____
2. sent	_____	6. clipped	_____
3. kicked	_____	7. bleed	_____
4. nut	[nʌt]	8. hummed	_____

C. Transcribe these IPA symbols into English words.

1. [dʌd] _____ 6. [bɛndz] _____

2. [dɛt] _____ 7. ['dɛd lɪ] _____

3. [tɛst] _____ 8. [stɪp] _____

4. [trɛk] _____ 9. [drɛdz] _____

5. [drɛst] _____ 10. [ə 'drɛst] _____

D. Vocalizations. Sing the following musical patterns, articulating each [t] and [d] clearly and easily.

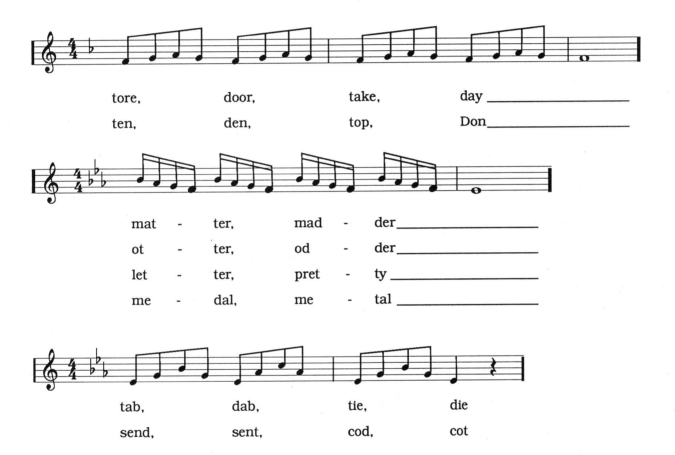

| tore, | door, | take, | day _____ |
| ten, | den, | top, | Don _____ |

mat - ter,	mad - der _____
ot - ter,	od - der _____
let - ter,	pret - ty _____
me - dal,	me - tal _____

| tab, | dab, | tie, | die |
| send, | sent, | cod, | cot |

E. Sentences with [t] and [d].

Read aloud these sentences, articulating quickly, easily and flexibly.

Tiny tots attain terribly, tattered mittens.

Doleful David disavows dapper Dan's disclaimer.

Exercises

The stop-plosive consonants [k] and [g]

Description

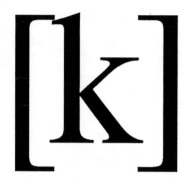

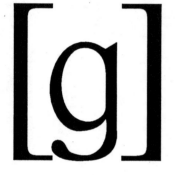

IPA Symbol	**[k]**	**[g]**
Word Example	*kit*	*gave*
Voicing	unvoiced	voiced
Place of Articulation	back of tongue and soft palate	
Manner of Articulation	stop-plosive The air flow stops as the back of the tongue lifts to touch the soft palate, closing off the oral passageway, and the soft palate is raised, closing off the nasal passageway. Air is then plosively released by the quick downward movement of the back of the tongue.	

Common Problems

The substitution of unvoiced **[k]** for voiced **[g]**, particularly when it is in the final position. *Vigor* should not sound like *vicar.*

The omission of **[k]** and **[g]**, which occurs most often in medial or final position as in *deck, beg,* or *arctic.*

Incomplete closure causing muffledness as in *deck* or *tact.*

Pressured articulation, building up too much pressure on the stop part of the stop-plosives **[k]** and **[g]**.

A. Articulation drills for [k] and [g].

Articulate the **[k]** and **[g]** consonants by lifting the back of the tongue to touch the soft palate. Keep the tip of the tongue behind the bottom front teeth and the jaw relaxed.

Read aloud these sounds.

Practice the following sounds in isolation to contrast the voiced and unvoiced qualities of each. Place your fingers on the front of your throat, on the Adam's apple, and say these sounds. Feel the vibration that occurs for **[g]** but not for **[k]**.

[k]   [g]   [k k]   [g g]   [k k k]   [g g g]

As you read these sounds, give attention to their precise, clean articulation while avoiding pressure or tightness in the throat. Keep the jaw relaxed.

[k]   [g]   [k k]   [g g]   [k k k]   [g g g]

Read aloud these paired words to contrast the sounds of **[k]** and **[g]**.

[k]	[g]
back	bag
Huck	hug
rack	rag
lack	lag
uncle	bungle
vicar	vigor
pick	pig
arc	Margaret
arctic	signify
tactic	significance

B. Transcribe these words with [k] and [g] into IPA symbols.

Read aloud the words as you write, clearly articulating each [k] and [g].

Initial

1. class _____   4. grime _____

2. glass _____   5. cane _____

3. crime _____   6. gain _____

Medial

1. racket _____   4. wigs _____

2. ragged _____   5. accident _____

3. wicks _____   6. mix _____

Final

1. pique _____   4. lug _____

2. pig _____   5 ask _____

3. luck _____   6 morgue _____

In our language, the letter *x* is transcribed as [ks] or [gz]. Listen carefully to your pronunciations.

fix [fɪks]   exalt [ɪg 'zɔlt]

excellent ['ɛk sə lənt]   exotic [ɪg 'zɑ tɪk]

C. Transcribe these IPA symbols into English words.

1. ['ɛg nɔg] _____   6. [glæd] _____

2. [læk] _____   7. [klɪpt] _____

3. [gɛst] _____   8. ['sɪks tɪ] _____

4. [kɪks] _____   9. [ə'grid] _____

5. [kɛgz] _____   10. ['ʌg lɪ] _____

D. Vocalize, articulating each [k] and [g] clearly and easily.

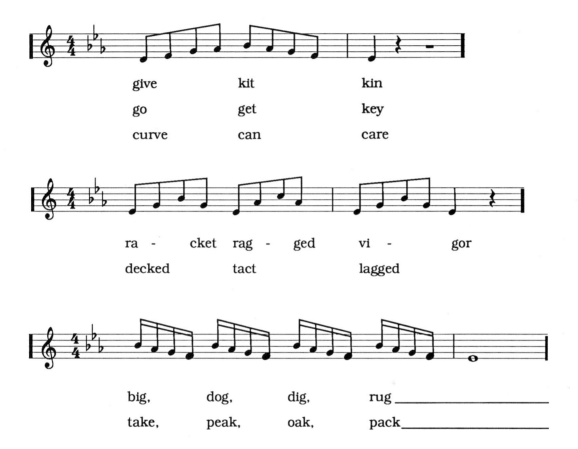

give   kit   kin

go   get   key

curve   can   care

ra - cket rag - ged vi - gor

decked   tact   lagged

big, dog, dig, rug _____

take, peak, oak, pack _____

E. Sentences with [k] and [g].

Read aloud these sentences, articulating quickly, easily and flexibly.

Ken's calm cow comforted Kathie's kicking, crying calves.

Good girls get great gag gifts.

IPA for Singers

Chapter 9 Worksheet

Transcribe these words into IPA symbols.

1. apostrophe — [ə'pɑstrəfi]
2. style — ['stɑɪ]
3. operate — ['ɑpəreɪt]
4. fundamental — [fʌndə'mɛntəl]
5. chords — ['kɔrdz]
6. kaleidoscope — [kə'lɑɪdəskɑrp]
7. except — [ɪks'ɛpt]
8. poetry — ['poʊətri]
9. resonated — ['rɛzəneɪtɪd]
10. baritone — ['bɛrə.toʊn]
11. baroque — [bə'roʊk]
12. mystic — ['mɪstɪk]
13. composer — [kəm'poʊzər]
14. duet — [du'ɛt]
15. expanded — [ɪks'pændəd]
16. discipline — ['dɪsəplən]
17. Gregorian — [grə'gɔriən]
18. actor — ['æktər]
19. triad — ['trɑɪæd]
20. polyphonic — [pɑlɪfɑnɪk]
21. trio — ['trioʊ]
22. melody — ['mɛlədi]
23. sustain — [sə'steɪn]
24. tenor — ['tɛnər]
25. gargle — ['gɑrgəl]
26. cue — [kju]
27. contralto — [kɑntr'æltoʊ]
28. piano — [pi'ænoʊ]
29. applause — [ə'plɔz]
30. accompanist — [ə'kʌmpənəst]

Transcribe these IPA symbols into English words.

1. ['glɑtɪs] — glotis
2. ['klæsɪk] — classic
3. [ˌbɪblɪ'ɑgrəfɪ] — bibliography
4. ['sɪmbəˌlɪzəm] — symbolism
5. ['oʊvərˌtoʊnz] — overtones
6. [ˌæk'sɛptəbəl] — acceptable
7. ['dɑmənənt] — dominant
8. ['tɑnɪk] — tonic
9. [sɔft 'pælɪt] — soft pallate
10. [lɪps] — lips
11. ['leɪbɪəl] — labial
12. ['pɑlɪps] — polyps
13. ['ɑktɪv] — active
14. ['plɔzəbəl] — plausible
15. ['pluˈrəl] — plural
16. [gʌlf] — gulf
17. [juzd] — used
18. ['stʌdɪ] — study
19. [dɪ'noʊt] — denote
20. ['beɪsˌbɔl] — baseball

146

CHAPTER 10
THE
NASAL
CONSONANTS

A nasal consonant is one in which the oral passageway is blocked at some point and the soft palate is lowered to allow the air to flow through the nasal passageway. There are only three nasal consonants in English:

[m] as in *me*

[n] as in *neat*

ng [ŋ] as in *hung*

[m]   [n]   [ŋ]

The soft palate is lowered, permitting air to enter nasal cavity

The soft palate is raised, closing the nasal passageway.

Exercises

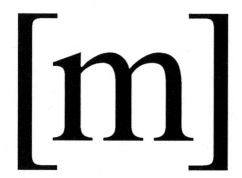

Description

The nasal consonant [m]

IPA Symbol	[m]
Word Example	*me*
Voicing	voiced
Place of Articulation	both lips
Manner of Articulation	nasal The lips close to stop the flow of air through the oral passageway. The soft palate lowers to permit air to flow through the nasal passageway. The tongue tip touches the back of the bottom front teeth.

Common problems

Insufficient nasal resonance. The [m] sound should be well hummed up through the nose in speech as well as singing.

Inadequate duration causing muffledness.

A. Articulation drills for [m].

The nasal sounds are long sounds. They give good resonance to the voice—brilliant tone and carrying power. Take advantage of them. Don't cheat them.

The consonant [m] vibrates fully when the cheeks are soft, the lips gently close, the jaw is relaxed with the teeth slightly separated, and the tongue is forward in the mouth.

Sing, using a vibrant [m] sound.

Sing the word *fume* [fjum] in slow motion: *ffffyyyyuuummmmmmm*. The *yot* [j] sound will help you bring your tongue forward. The rounded [u] will help you relax your jaw by bringing your lips forward. As you close your lips for the [m], feel that you are gathering the vibration of the [u] into the [m]. The sustained [m] should feel and sound vibrant and buzzy. Sing on a pitch in your speaking range for this exercise.

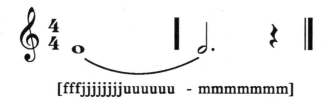

[fffjjjjjjjjjuuuuuu - mmmmmmm]

Read aloud these words.

With your lips lightly touching each other, sustain the sound of each [m] for four full counts. Feel the vibration of sound in the front of the face, around the lips or nose. Do not force the sound nor allow it to fade in intensity. Maintain adequate breath support during all four counts.

Counts: 1 2 3 4   1 2 3 4

Say:

summer (summmmmmmmer)   hem (hemmmmmmmm)

hammer (hammmmmmmmer)   I'm (I'mmmmmmmm)

somewhere (sommmmmewhere)   game (gammmmmmme)

humble (hummmmmmmmble)   dumb (dummmmmmmb)

Read aloud these words.

Linger over the [m] sound in each word, letting it "sing out" in speech with the same vibrance as in singing.

yam	amplify
storm	prompt
came	warmth
bottom	resembles
hum	thimble
some	pumped
perform	formulate
from	comfort
tomb	complicated
rhythm	rumble

B. Transcribe these words into IPA symbols.

Read aloud the words as you write. Be sure each [m] vibrates clearly and easily.

Initial

1. me   [mi]   4. mop _____

2. moo _____ 5. merry _____

3. must _____ 6. mire _____

Medial

1. hammer_____ 4. bloomed _____

2. army _____ 5. blamed _____

3. summer_____ 6. timid _____

Final

1. name _____ 4. some _____

2. I'm _____ 5. Rome _____

3. sum _____ 6. team _____

C. Transcribe these IPA symbols into English words.

1. [slɪm] _____ 6. [kleɪm] _____

2. [maɪt] _____ 7. ['kɑ mən] _____

3. ['traɪ əmf] _____ 8. ['mju zɪk] _____

4. [ɪk 'strim]_____ 9. [praɪm] _____

5. [tum] _____ 10. [maʊs] _____

D. Vocalizing with [m], vibrating each [m] clearly and easily.

Humming with [m].

mmmmmmmmmmmmmmmm

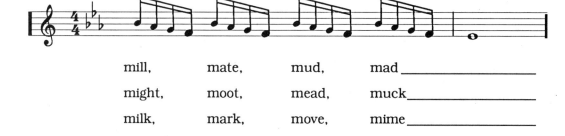

mill,	mate,	mud,	mad _____
might,	moot,	mead,	muck_____
milk,	mark,	move,	mime_____

comf - ort,	farm - er,	tam - er,	aimed
lim - ber,	calm - er,	clum - sy,	named
sum - mer,	dumb - er,	room - er,	homed

some	seem	slam	Sam
deem	dumb	dam	dame
him	ham	home	I'm

E. Sentences with [m].

Read aloud these sentences, vibrating each [m] clearly and easily.

Managing the menu made Mary moan.

Mirthful music maintains many men.

Exercises

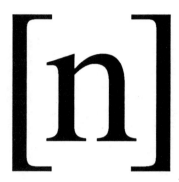

The nasal consonant [n]

Description

IPA Symbol	[n]
Word Example	_n_eat
Voicing	voiced
Place of Articulation	teeth ridge and tongue tip
Manner of Articulation	nasal The tongue tip touches the teeth ridge to stop the flow of air through the oral cavity. The soft palate lowers to permit air to pass through the nasal cavity.

Common problems

Insufficient nasal resonance. The [n] sound should be well hummed up through the nose for speech as well as singing.

Inadequate duration causing muffledness.

A. Articulation drills for [n].

The consonant [n] can be fully vibrated when the tip of the tongue lifts to gently touch the teeth ridge and teeth. Let your jaw drop slightly. As you say [n], feel the vibrations at the tip of the tongue. The sound of the sustained [n] is a hum, just as the [m] is a hum.

Sing, using a vibrating [n] hum.

Sing the word *funeral* ['fju nə rəl] in slow motion: *fyyyuunnnnnnnnnnnnnnnnnneral*. Pause on the *n* [n] sound. Feel the lifted tongue tip gently touch your teeth ridge. Listen for the vibrant hum.

The nasal sounds are long sounds, providing good resonance to the voice—brilliant tone and carrying power. Take advantage of them. Don't cheat them.

[fffjjjuuuunnnnnnnnnnnnnnnnn] ......

Read aloud these words.

With your tongue tip lightly touching the teeth ridge, sustain each [n] sound for four full counts. Feel the vibration which occurs around the tip of the tongue and the nose. Do not force the sound nor allow it to fade in intensity. Maintain adequate breath support during all four counts.

Counts: 1 2 3 4   1 2 3 4

Say:

tender (tennnnnnnder)	pin (pinnnnnnnn)
handy (hannnnnnnndy)	town (townnnnnn)
canyon (cannnnnnyon	crane (crannnnnne)
spent (spennnnnnnt)	brain (brainnnnn)

Linger over the [n] sound in each word, letting it "sing out" in speech with the same vibrancy as in singing.

sinner	tint
loosen	sender
sound	content
pen	conversation
pound	range
throne	friend
groan	tones
counter	center

B. Transcribe these words into IPA symbols.

Read the words aloud as you write. Vibrate each [n] clearly and easily.

Initial

1. note	[noʊt]	4. nail	_____
2. knock	_____	5. neat	_____
3. nip	_____	6. nice	_____

Medial

1. bundle	_____	4. annul	_____
2. tenor	_____	5. mental	_____
3. invent	_____	6. donor	_____

Final

1. man	_____	4. brown	_____
2. moon	_____	5. stun	_____
3. in	_____	6. fan	_____

C. Transcribe these IPA symbols into English words.

1. [nus]	_____	6. ['trænz ˌleɪt]	_____
2. [naɪt]	_____	7. [ˌʌn 'lʌ kɪ]	_____
3. [ˌʌn 'dʌn]	_____	8. [nun]	_____
4. [rɛnt]	_____	9. ['nɪf tɪ]	_____
5. [dreɪnd]	_____	10. [ˌʌn 'taɪ]	_____

D. Vocalize, vibrating each [n] clearly and easily.

nnnnnnnnnnnnnnnnnnnnnnnnnnnnnnnnnnnnnnnnnnnnnnnn

not	know	name
knee	Nick	night
neat	noon	nap

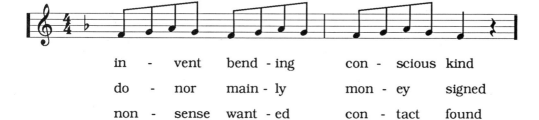

in - vent	bend - ing	con - scious	kind
do - nor	main - ly	mon - ey	signed
non - sense	want - ed	con - tact	found

gone	den	green
fun	done	can
own	won	ton

E. Sentences with [n].

Read aloud these sentences, vibrating each **[n]** clearly and easily.

Ned's new neighbors never need noisy nights.

Nanny found invitations were not necessary.

Exercises

The nasal consonant *ng* [ŋ]
[ŋ] is called *eng* [ɛŋ]

Description

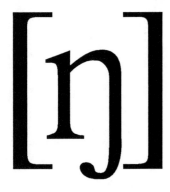

IPA Symbol	[ŋ]
Word Example	*hung*
Voicing	voiced
Place of Articulation	back of tongue and soft palate
Manner of Articulation	nasal The back of the tongue is raised to touch the soft palate and stop the flow of air through the oral passageway. The soft palate lowers to permit air to pass through the nasal cavity.

Common problems

Insufficient nasal resonance. The [ŋ] sound should be well hummed up through the nose.

Inadequate duration causing muffledness. The nasal consonants are long sounds. Be sure to give them adequate duration.

Substitution of [n] for [ŋ], particularly in *ing* words. *Coming* becomes *comin'*.

A. Articulation drills for [ŋ].

Take advantage of the [ŋ] hum for good resonance—brilliant tone and carrying power. Don't cut short the duration of this sound.

Read aloud these words.

With the back of your tongue gently touching the soft palate, sustain each *ng* [ŋ] for four full counts. Relax your throat and feel the sound vibrate around your nose. Do not force the sound nor allow it to fade in intensity. Maintain adequate breath support during all four counts.

In these examples, sustain the consonant ng [ŋ], not the vowels.

Counts:	1 2 3 4		1 2 3 4
Say:	sing		spring ....
	going		coming ....
	tongue		king ....

Pronounce "ing" with ih [ɪ], as in coming [kʌm ɪŋ], not ee [i] as in [kʌm iŋ].

Read aloud these words using *ng* [ŋ]. Notice that there is no [g] sound in these words.

hanging	['hæŋ ɪŋ] not ['hæŋg ɪŋ]
sing a song	[sɪŋ ə sɔŋ]
singing	['sɪŋ ɪŋ]
hanger	['hæŋ ər]
swinging	['swɪŋ ɪŋ]
Long Island	[lɔŋ 'aɪ lənd]

Read aloud these words spelled with *ng*. These words are pronounced with [ŋ] plus the consonant [g].

finger	['fɪŋ gər]
single	['sɪŋ gəl]
elongate	[ɪ 'lɔŋ ˌgeɪt]
spangled	['spæŋ gəld]
stronger	['strɔŋ gər]

Read aloud these words spelled with *nk*, *nc* or *nx*. These words are pronounced with [ŋ] plus the consonant [k].

bank	[bæŋk]
drunk	[drʌŋk]
tanks	[tæŋks]
ankle	['æŋ kəl]
anchor	['æŋ kər]
Lincoln	['lɪŋ kən]

Read aloud these paired words to contrast the [n] and [ŋ] sounds. Feel the difference between tongue positions for [n] and [ŋ]. For [n] the tip of the tongue lifts to touch the teeth ridge. For [ŋ] the back of the tongue lifts to touch the soft palate.

[n]	[ŋ]
sin	sing
sun	sung
ban	bang
bun	bungle
kin	king
lawn	long

Read aloud these words being careful not to substitute [n] for [ŋ]. The *ing* words in our language are particularly susceptible to this substitution.

coming	*not* comin'
practicing	*not* practicin'
nothing	*not* nothin'
being	*not* bein'
strength	*not* strenth
length	*not* lenth

B. Transcribe these words into IPA symbols.

Read the words aloud as you write. Vibrate each [ŋ] clearly and easily. Notice there is no initial position for this consonant in English.

Medial

1. singer ['sɪŋər]   4. angular _____

2. monkey _____   5. strongly _____

3. tingle _____   6. larynx _____

Final

1. hung _____   4. song _____

2. long _____   5. among _____

3. bring _____   6. ring _____

C. Transcribe these IPA symbols into English words.

1. [bæŋ] _____   6. ['swɪŋ ər] _____

2. [ræŋ] _____   7. ['du ɪŋ] _____

3. [brɪŋk] _____   8. [gæŋ] _____

4. [sæŋ] _____   9. ['rɪd ɪŋ] _____

5. [tɔŋz] _____   10. [wɪŋ] _____

D. Vocalize, vibrating each [ŋ] clearly and easily.

[ŋ --]

sing	-	er
bun	-	gle
hang	-	ar
fling	-	ing

ring	rang	rung _____
sing	sang	sung _____
long	flung	strong _____
see - ing		giv - ing

pin	ping	sin	sing
flint	fling	lone	long
togs	tongs	brick	brink
black	blank	tug	tongue
log	long	duck	dunk

Articulate carefully the consonants in these paired words.

E. Sentences with [ŋ].

Read aloud these sentences, vibrating each [ŋ] clearly and easily.

Frank longs to sing a soaring song.
Young and single, they languish for strong dungarees.

Chapter 10 Worksheet

Transcribe these words into IPA symbols.

1. sustain   [sə'steɪn]
2. harmony   ['har məni]
3. nasal   ['neɪ zəl]
4. symphony   ['sɪm fəni]
5. contemporary   [kən 'tɛm pər ɛri]

6. monotone   ['manə toʊn]
7. singer   ['sɪ ŋər]
8. dressing room   ['drɛsɪŋ rum]
9. training   [treɪ nɪŋ]
10. consonants   ['kan sənənts]

11. pharynx   ['fɛ rɪŋks]
12. unison   ['ju nəsən]
13. monologue   ['manə lɔg]
14. dramatic   [drə 'mætɪk]
15. manuscript   ['mæn jə skrɪpt]

16. prolong   [prə 'lɔŋ]
17. starring   ['sta rɪŋ]
18. tongue   [tʌ ŋ]
19. mandolin   [mæn də lɪn]
20. make-up   ['meɪ kʌp]

21. announce   [ə'n aʊ ns]
22. season   ['si zən]
23. interview   ['ɪn tər vju]
24. dancer   ['dæn sər]
25. velum   ['vɛ lʊm]

26. winning   [wɪ nɪŋ]
27. inspiring   [ɪn'spaɪ rɪŋ]
28. tempo   ['tɛm poʊ]
29. meter   ['mi tər]
30. heroine   [hɛ roʊən]

Transcribe these IPA symbols into English words.

1. ['læ rɪŋks]   larynx
2. [sə'nɔ rə tɪ]   sonority
3. ['stju dənts]   students
4. ['tɪm pə ni]   timpani
5. ['daɪ ə fræm]   diapragm

6. [mɔɪst]
7. [flɛm]
8. ['saɪ nəs]
9. [ɪn 'tɛn sə tɪ]
10. ['æb də mən]

11. ['dɛn təl]
12. ['tjun ɪŋ]
13. [ɪn 'toʊn]
14. ['freɪ zɪŋ]
15. ['krun ɪŋ]
16. [slæŋ]
17. ['noʊ bəl]
18. ['sɑ nɪt]
19. ['daɪn ɪŋ]
20. ['læf ɪŋ]

Chapter 11
The Fricative Consonants

A fricative consonant is one in which the air flow is partially interrupted as it passes through the vocal tract, thus producing a noisy sound. Fricatives are longer sounds than the short stop-plosives. Because they can be sustained, they are called *continuants*. The fricative consonants in English are:

    1. The cognates [f] as in *feet* and [v] as in *vain*.

    2. The "th" cognates: [θ] as in *think* and [ð] as in *then*.

    3. The cognates [s] as in *sea* and [z] as in *zip*.

    4. The "sh" and "zh" cognates: [ʃ] as in *she* and [ʒ] as in *azure*.

    5. The consonant [h] as in *heat*.

$$[f] \quad [v] \quad [\theta] \quad [ð]$$

$$[s] \quad [z] \quad [ʃ] \quad [ʒ]$$

$$[h]$$

Exercises

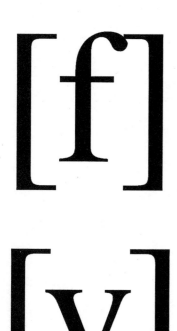

The fricative consonants [f] and [v]

Description

IPA Symbol	**[f]**	**[v]**
Word Example	*feet*	*vain*
Voicing	unvoiced	voiced
Place of Articulation	upper teeth and lower lip	
Manner of Articulation	fricative The lower lip gently touches the upper teeth. Air is forced out between the lower lip and upper teeth. The soft palate is raised, closing the nasal passageway.	

Common problems

Pressured articulation. Many people speak these consonants in a pressured way, so that they sound more like a stop-plosive consonant rather than a sustained fricative.

The omission of **[f]** and **[v]**, particularly before other consonants (*give me* becomes *gimme*).

The substitution of unvoiced **[f]** for voiced **[v]**. The word *have* becomes *haf*.

A. Articulation drills for [f] and [v].

When articulating **[f]** and **[v]**, listen for the sustained fricative sound which is produced by the escaping air between the lower lip and upper teeth. Be careful not to press or force the sound. It should be a gentle sound. Building up too much force will create unnecessary throat tension.

Read aloud these sounds.

Practice the following sounds in isolation to contrast the voiced and unvoiced qualities of each. Place a finger on the front of your throat, on the Adam's apple, and say the following. Feel the vibration that occurs for **[v]** but not for **[f]**.

Keep in mind that voiced consonants have pitch.

[f] [v] [f f] [v v] [f f f] [v v v]

Sustain the sound of the fricative consonants **[f]** and **[v]** for the duration of two slow counts. Avoid pressured articulation.

Counts:	1 2		1 2
(feel)	fffffffffffffffeel	(veal)	vvvvvvveal
(fine)	ffffffffffffffffine	(vast)	vvvvvvvvast
(self)	selfffffffffffffff	(rave)	ravvvvvvvvvve
(fool)	fffffffffffffffool	(vile)	vvvvvvvvvile
(if)	iffffffffffffffffff	(believe)	believvvvvvvvvve

Read aloud these words, being careful not to omit the **[f]** and **[v]** sounds.

Give me that. (Not *Gimme that*).

What a golf course!

Love me or leave me.

Graph paper.

Read aloud these words to contrast the sounds of **[f]** and **[v]**. Do not substitute **[f]** for **[v]**, but give full voicing to each **[v]**.

safe - save

leaf - leave

half - have

B. Transcribe into IPA symbols these words with [f] and [v] .

Read aloud the words as you write. Articulate each [f] and [v] clearly and easily.

Initial

1. feet [fit]   4. fat _____

2. vail [veɪl]   5. vat _____

3. fail _____   6. vim _____

Medial

1. affair _____   4. reveal _____

2. differ _____   5. drafty _____

3. lever _____   6. over _____

Final

1. rave _____   4. reef _____

2. cough _____   5. rough _____

3. stove _____   6. self _____

C. Transcribe these IPA symbols into English words.

1. [hæf] _____   6. [kæf] _____

2. [hævz] _____   7. [dɪ 'fɛkt] _____

3. [grif] _____   8. [loʊf] _____

4. [grivz] _____   9. [loʊvz] _____

5. ['fi vər] _____ 10. ['læf tər] _____

D. Vocalize, articulating each [f] and [v] clearly and easily.

vvvvvvvvvvvvvvvvvvvvvvvvvvvvvvvvvvv

vote	fore	vice	fight
forge	vogue	fan	van
vase	feign	vault	fault

tough - er	fer - vor	hav - ing
draft - y	pave - ment	ri - fle
heav - y	craft - y	dri - ver

cuff	cove	waif	wave _____
prove	proof	strife	strive _____
cliff	give	leaf	leave _____
safe	save	serve	surf _____

E. Sentences with [f] and [v].

Read aloud these sentences, articulating [f] and [v] clearly and easily.

Few fellows feign fine feelings.

Voodoo vendors vowed vast vocal viruses.

Exercises

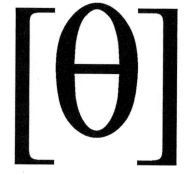

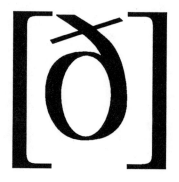

The *th* consonants [θ] and [ð]
[θ] is called by its sound or by the name *theta*
[θetə]. [ð] is called by its sound or by the name
ethe* [εð] or *crossed d.

Description

IPA Symbol	[θ] theta	[ð] ethe
Word Example	*think* *faith*	*then* *smooth*
Voicing	unvoiced	voiced
Place of Articulation	upper front teeth and tongue	
Manner of Articulation	fricative The upper front teeth and tongue touch. Air passes between the tongue blade and upper teeth. The sides of the tongue touch the upper molars. The soft palate is raised, closing the nasal passageway.	

Common problems

The substitution of unvoiced [θ] for voiced [ð]. *Teethe* must not sound like *teeth*.

Misarticulation by putting the tip of the tongue behind the teeth resulting in a sound like a stop-plosive [t] or [d]. *These* should not sound like *dese*.

The omission of [θ] or [ð], particularly in consonant clusters.

Inadequate duration of the sounds of [θ] and [ð] resulting in muffledness.

A. Articulation drills for [θ] and [ð].

Listen for the sustained fricative sound of [θ] and [ð]. Be careful not to press or force the sound. Building up too much force will create unnecessary tongue and throat tension.

Read aloud these sounds.

Practice the following sounds in isolation to contrast the voiced and unvoiced qualities of each. Place your hand on the front of your throat, on the Adam's apple, and say the following sounds. Feel the vibration that occurs for *ethe* [ð] but not for *theta* [θ].

Remember that voiced consonants, such as ethe, [ð], *have pitch.*

[θ] [ð]

[θ θ]   [ð ð]

[θ ð θ]   [θ ð θ]

Read these words aloud, sustaining the sound of each *theta* [θ] and *ethe* [ð] for the duration of a full measure. Avoid forcing or pressuring the sounds. Sustain the consonants, not the vowel.

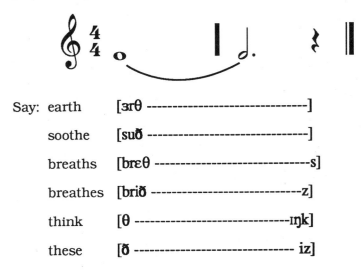

Say:	earth	[ɝθ ---------------------------]
	soothe	[suð ---------------------------]
	breaths	[brɛθ ---------------------------s]
	breathes	[brið ---------------------------z]
	think	[θ ---------------------------ɪŋk]
	these	[ð --------------------------- iz]

Read aloud these words. Be careful not to omit the *theta* [θ] and *ethe* [ð] sounds.

both of them

bathe a child

width   [wɪdθ] or [wɪtθ]

breadth   [brɛdθ] or [brɛtθ]

B. Transcribe into IPA symbols these words using *theta* [θ] and *ethe* [ð].

Read aloud the words as you write, articulating each [θ] and [ð] clearly and easily. If you are unsure about the voicing, sustain the "th" for two slow counts. This will help you distinguish between [θ] and [ð].

Initial

1. these [ðiz]   4. thine _____

2. thin [θɪn]   5. third _____

3. there _____   6. them _____

Medial

1. rather _____   4. father _____

2. method _____   5. weather _____

3. ethics _____   6. broth _____

Final

1. path _____   4. breath _____

2. writhe _____   5 breathe _____

3. beneath _____   6. soothe _____

C. Transcribe these IPA symbols into English words.

1. [ðɪs] _____   6. [sɪð] _____

2. [θri] _____   7. [mʌnθ] _____

3. [leɪð] _____   8. [ræθ] _____

4. [mɪθs] _____   9. ['skeɪ ðɪŋ] _____

5. ['θɪm bəl] _____   10. [ðɛr] _____

D.Vocalize, articulating each [θ] and [ð] clearly and easily.

[ð -------------------------------------]

think	thick	thaw	thank
thee	then	thine	this
thumb	there	thin	these
through	them	they	that

either	mother	rather	noth	-	ing
method	author	feather	oth	-	er
father	earthy	breathy	teeth	--	ing

myth	troth	lath
bathe	clothe	lathe
path	tooth	both
smooth	breathe	writhe

E. Sentences with [θ] and [ð].

Read aloud the following sentences, articulating clearly and easily.

Ethical thinkers think ethereal, thrilling, truthful, faithful thoughts.

This worthy bathing soothes the father in seething, writhing, scathing weather.

Exercises

The fricative consonants [s] and [z]

Description

[s]

[z]

IPA Symbol	[s]	[z]
Word Example	*sea* *ra_ce_*	*zip* *wa_s_*
Voicing	unvoiced	voiced
Place of Articulation	tip or blade of tongue near teeth ridge	
Manner of Articulation	fricative Either the tip of the tongue is near the teeth ridge <u>or</u> the blade of the tongue is near the teeth ridge with the tip behind the bottom front teeth. Air flows between the teeth and tongue. Sides of the tongue touch the upper molars. Soft palate is raised, closing nasal passageway.	

Common problems

Frontal and lateral lisps.

The substitution of unvoiced [s] for voiced [z]. *Ribs* must not sound like *rips*.

A. Articulation drills for [s] and [z].

The fricative consonants [s] and [z] are created by the exiting air through the center of the mouth over the tongue tip or blade. The tongue can be placed in either of two positions, both of which have the same acoustic result. One way is to suspend the tip of the tongue in the front of the mouth near the teeth ridge. The other is to place the tip of the tongue behind the back of the bottom teeth and raise the blade of the tongue toward the teeth ridge. Both of these tongue placements produce a clear [s] or [z]. Notice which way you make [s] and [z].

Read aloud the following sounds to contrast the voiced and unvoiced qualities of each. Place your hand on the front of your throat, on your Adam's apple, and say the following sounds. Feel the vibration that occurs for [z] but not for [s].

[s]   [z]   [s s]   [z z]   [s s s]   [z z z]

Read aloud these words to contrast [s] and [z].

[s]	[z]
sip	zip
sag	zag
sink	zinc
lacy	lazy
price	prize
false	falls
rice	rise
lacks	lags
waltz	walls
beets	beads

Read aloud these words avoiding pressured articulation. Sustain the sound of each fricative [s] and [z] for the duration of two slow counts.

Counts: 1 2   1 2

(pass) passsssssss   (rise) risssssssssse

(seal) sssssssssseal   (zeal) *zzzzzzzzzzzz*eal

Read aloud these paired words to contrast [θ] - [s] and [ð] - [z].

In the following words feel the contrast as the tongue moves from between the teeth for the sounds [θ] and [ð] to the back of the teeth in the following words for the [s] and [z] sounds.

[θ]	[s]	[ð]	[z]
bath	bass	bathe	bays
myth	miss	breathe	breeze
path	pass	seethe	seize
thank	sank	withered	wizard
theme	seem	writhing	rising

A frontal lisp occurs when some people produce [s] and [z] with their tongue tip inappropriately placed between the teeth like a "th" sound.

A lateral lisp occurs when air escapes around the sides of the tongue rather than over the center and the tongue tip. The tip is pressed firmly against the teeth ridge and the corners of the lips are often pulled back to permit the escape of air.

Read aloud these words to increase your tactile awareness of the placement of the tongue. Repeat the word *eat* several times until you feel the firm contact of the sides of the tongue with the teeth. As you repeat the words below, adding [s] or [z], keep the sides of the tongue lifted. Listen for a sharp quality of the [s] and [z] when emitted properly from the front of the mouth.

eat - eats - eats - eatsss - eatssss [sssssss]

tote - totes - totes - totesss - totessss [ssssssss]

bead - beads - beads - beadsss - beadssss [zzzzzzz]

toad - toads - toads - toadsss - toadssss [zzzzzzzz]

B. Transcribe into IPA symbols these words using [s] and [z] .

Read aloud the words as you write, articulating the [s] and [z] clearly and easily. If you are unsure about the voicing, sustain the sound for two slow counts. This should help you distinguish between [s] and [z].

Initial

1. soap [soʊp]   5. sleep _____
2. zeal [zil]   6. zoom _____
3. sin _____   7. sane _____
4. zebra _____   8. zip _____

Medial

1. puzzle _____   5. music _____
2. abysmal _____   6. freezer _____
3. misty _____   7. thirsty _____
4. pencil _____   8. thistle _____

Final

1. rose _____   5. these _____
2. pass _____   6. this _____
3. lags _____   7. bets _____
4. peace _____   8. beds _____

C. Transcribe these IPA Symbols into English words.

1. [sɔt] _____   6. [kloʊz] _____
2. [zoʊn] _____   7. [kloʊs] _____
3. ['zɪ nɪθ] _____   8. [sis] _____
4. [saʊnd] _____   9. [siz] _____
5. [dɪ 'fjuz] _____   10. [piz] _____

D. Vocalize with [s] and [z]:

ZZZZZZZZZZZZZZZZZZZZZZZZZZZZZZZZZZZZZZ

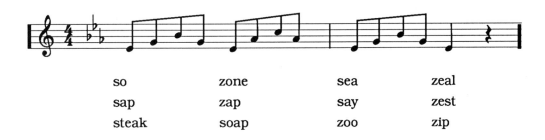

so	zone	sea	zeal
sap	zap	say	zest
steak	soap	zoo	zip

rac - er	mer - cy	pass - ing
haz - y	los - er	diz - zy
eas - y	froz - en	fac - ing

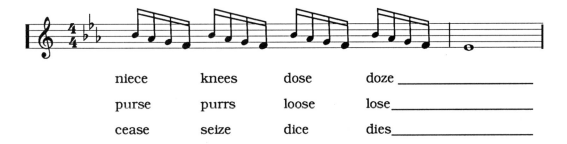

niece	knees	dose	doze _____
purse	purrs	loose	lose_____
cease	seize	dice	dies_____

E. Sentences with [s] and [z].

Read aloud the following sentences, articulating [s] and [z] clearly and easily.

Sam said Sandra saw several Soviet submarines.

His dazzling roses cause cosmic breezes.

Exercises

The sh and zh fricative consonants [ʃ] and [ʒ]
[ʃ] is called esh [ɛʃ].
[ʒ] is called by its sound, as in _azure_.

Description

[ʃ]

[ʒ]

IPA Symbol	[ʃ] Called *esh* [ɛʃ]	[ʒ] Called by its sound
Word Example	*she* o*c*ean *sugar* na*ti*on	*azure* ca*s*ual bei*g*e
Voicing	unvoiced	voiced
Place of Articulation	tongue blade and boundary of the teeth ridge and hard palate	
Manner of Articulation	fricative The sides of the tongue laterally touch the side teeth. The tongue tip is pointed either toward the back of the teeth ridge or lower gum ridge. Air shoots out over the tongue and between the front teeth.The soft palate is raised, closing the nasal passagewaay.	

Common problems

Lateral lisp, in which air escapes over the sides of the tongue rather than over the center.

The substitution of unvoiced *esh* [ʃ] for voiced [ʒ]. (*Fission* should not rhyme with *vision*.)

A. Articulation drills for *esh* [ʃ] and [ʒ].

Read aloud the following sounds to contrast the voiced and unvoiced qualities of each. Place your hand on the front of your throat, on the Adam's apple, as you say the following sounds. Feel the vibration that occurs for [ʒ] but not for *esh* [ʃ].

[ʃ]   [ʒ]   [ʃ ʒ]   [ʒ ʒ]   [ʃ ʃ ʒ]   [ʒ ʒ ʒ]

Read aloud the following words to contrast the sounds of *esh* [ʃ] and [ʒ]. Give full voicing to each [ʒ].

[ʃ]	[ʒ]
fi<u>ss</u>ion	vi<u>s</u>ion
cau<u>ti</u>on	ca<u>s</u>ual
lu<u>sc</u>ious	fu<u>s</u>ion
pa<u>ss</u>ion	presti<u>g</u>e
an<u>xi</u>ous	gara<u>g</u>e

Read aloud these sentences. If you have a particular kind of lisp on [s] and [z], you probably will have that problem with [ʃ] and [ʒ]. The most common is the *lateral lisp* where the air comes out over the sides of the tongue rather than over the center. Check your articulation of [ʃ] and [ʒ] in these sentences.

My dic<u>ti</u>on is good.

It is a ca<u>s</u>ual party.

My profe<u>ss</u>ion is teaching.

His vi<u>s</u>ion is broad.

Contrast final [ʒ] and [z].

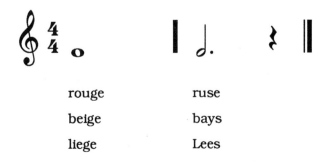

rouge	ruse
beige	bays
liege	Lees

B. Transcribe into IPA symbols these words using [ʃ] and [ʒ] .

Read aloud the words as you write, articulating each [ʃ] and [ʒ] clearly and easily. If you are unsure about the voicing, sustain the sound for two slow counts. This should help you distinguish between [ʃ] and [ʒ].

Initial

1. she   [ʃ i]   There is no initial [ʒ]
2. sure   _____   in English.
3. sheep   _____

Medial

1. ocean   _____   4. delusion [dɪ 'lu ʒən]
2. fraction _____   5. seizure   _____
3. assure   _____   6. visual   _____

Final

1. mash   _____   4. beige   _____
2. cash   _____   5. rouge   _____
3. thrash _____   6. prestige _____

C. Transcribe these IPA symbols into English words.

1. [rʌʃ]   _____   6. [ʃeɪm]   _____

2. [ʃɑt]   _____   7. [flɛʃ]   _____

3. [mɪ 'rɑʒ] _____   8. [gə 'rɑʒ] _____

4. [ə 'keɪ ʒən] _____ 9. ['vɪ ʒən] _____

5. ['ʃʊ gər] _____   10. ['kɔ ʃən] _____

D. Vocalize with [ʃ] and [ʒ].

| sheen | shot | sharp | shirk _____ |
| shout | sure | she | shut _____ |

| shake | sake | shame | same |
| shun | sun | sheet | see |

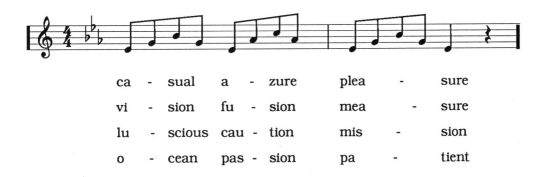

ca - sual	a - zure	plea - sure
vi - sion	fu - sion	mea - sure
lu - scious	cau - tion	mis - sion
o - cean	pas - sion	pa - tient

rush	rouge	bar - rage_____
cors - age	mi - rage_____
brash	gash	un - leash_____

E. Sentences with [ʃ] and [ʒ].

Read aloud the following sentences, articulating [ʃ] and [ʒ] clearly and easily.

Shepherds shouldn't shoot sheared sheep.

Unusual beige garages measure prestige.

Exercises

The fricative consonant [h]

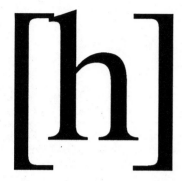

Description

IPA Symbol	[h]
Word Example	*heat*
Voicing	unvoiced
Place of Articulation	glottis
Manner of Articulation	fricative Air escapes unvoiced through the glottis (space between the vocal folds). The articulators are in position for the vowel which follows the [h]. The soft palate is raised, closing the nasal passageway.

Common problems

Over-aspiration, pushing too much air through the glottis resulting in breathiness.

A. Articulation drills for [h].

Read aloud, differentiating between these paired words, with and without an [h].

haste	aced
has	as
hear	ear
hate	ate
high	I
Hugh	you
who's	ooze

B. Transcribe into IPA symbols these words using [h].

The initial wh in the words who [hu], whole [hoʊl], and their derivatives are pronounced with [h]. Other words beginning with wh such as white and whither are pronounced with an unvoiced w [hw]. See Chapter 13 on Glides for a full discussion of [hw] and [w].

Initial

1. heat ___[hit]___   4. whole _____

2. hound _____   5. hammer _____

3. hue _____   6. home _____

Medial

1. ahead _____   4. antihistamine _____

2. unwholesome _____   5. inhuman _____

3. inheritance _____   6. uphill _____

*In the words **hue** and **human** the initial h is pronounced in standard American speech. There is no final [h] sound in English.*

C. Transcribe these IPA symbols into English words.

1. [hæf] _____   6. [ˌæd 'hi sɪv] _____

2. [hɑt] _____   7. [ˌʌn 'hæ pɪ] _____

3. ['hɔ tɪ] _____   8. ['hi ðən] _____

4. [heɪl] _____   9. ['hju mən] _____

5. [hʌg] _____   10. [bɪ 'hɛd ɪd] _____

*In many spellings in English, h is not sounded, as in **honor** and **exhibit**. Listen carefully to your pronunciations.*

D. Vocalize with [h].

Practice the onset of tone using words with and without an [h].

ear	hear	as	has
old	whole	ate	hate

*The fricative consonant **[h]** is an unvoiced sound and cannot be sung. This sound is useful for vocalization by singers, however, to avoid a glottal plosive attack and to learn a gentle onset of tone.*

E. Sentences with [h].

Read aloud the following sentence, articulating the [h] clearly and easily.

He who has high hopes humors humanity.

Chapter 11 Worksheet

Transcribe these words into IPA symbols.

1. zest — [ˈzɛst]
2. witnesses — [ˈwɪt nəsəz]
3. patronize — [ˈpeɪ trənaɪz]
4. nasal — [ˈneɪ zəl]
5. sextet — [sɛks ˈtɛt]

6. shallow — [ˈʃæ loʊ]
7. leisure — [ˈlɛʒ ər]
8. haberdasher — _____
9. nation — [neɪ ʃən]
10. immersion — [ɪ'mɜr ʒən]

11. thwart — [θwɔrt]
12. hourly — [aʊ rli]
13. loathe — [loʊ ð]
14. loath — [loʊ θ]
15. invert — [ˈɪnvɜrt]

16. fling — [flɪŋ]
17. ghost — [goʊst]
18. headphone — [ˈhɛd foʊn]
19. entourage — [an tv ˈraʒ]
20. foreclosure — [fɔrˈkloʊʒər]

21. partial — [par ʃəl]
22. crazy — [ˈkreɪ zi]
23. medicine — [mɛ də sən]
24. valuable — [ˈvæ ljə bəl]
25. motherland — [ˈmʌð ər lænd]

26. exhaust — [ɪg ˈzast]
27. brethren — [ˈbrɛ ðrən]
28. mouth — [maʊ θ]
29. phonetic — [fəˈnɛtɪk]
30. cashew — [kæ ʃu]

Transcribe these IPA symbols into English words.

1. [ˈvou kə liz] _____
2. [ˈvou kə laɪz] _____
3. [flæt] _____
4. [ˈfeɪ məs] _____
5. [θrɪl] _____

6. [ˈnɛ ðər lændz] _____
7. [ˈhɑr mə nɪ] _____
8. [hɑrt] _____
9. [saʊθ] _____
10. [ɪn ˈhɪ bɪ tɪd] _____

11. [buθ] _____
12. [ˈfrɔ θɪ] _____
13. [ˈfou tə ˌgræf] _____
14. [vɪ ˈbrɑ ˌtou] _____
15. [tɪð] _____

16. [keɪv] _____
17. [ˈsæ ˌflaʊ ər] _____
18. [ˌnɔrθ ˈist] _____
19. [ˈheɪ vən] _____
20. [ˈhɛ vən] _____

Chapter 12
The
Lateral
Consonant
[l]

A lateral consonant is one in which the sides of the tongue are lowered, not touching the upper molars. The breath flows laterally over one or both sides of the tongue, and comes out the sides of the mouth. The [l] is the only lateral consonant in English.

[l]

Exercises

The lateral consonant [l]

Description

[l]

IPA Symbol	[l]
Word Example	*lift*
Voicing	voiced
Place of Articulation	tongue tip and teeth ridge
Manner of Articulation	lateral The tip of the tongue raises to touch the teeth ridge. The sides of the tongue lower to permit the flow of air over the sides of the tongue and out the sides of the mouth.

Common Problems

Slack articulation, occurring when the tongue tip does not firmly touch the teeth ridge, resulting in an indistinct, muffled sound.

The omission of [l], occurring most often in the medial positions. The word *help* should not become *hep* [hɛp]

Tongue thrust occurring when the speaker puts the tongue between the teeth to make [l]. The tip of the tongue tends to be pointed and tense.

In English there are four allophones of [l]. First, there is the clear [l] which is made with the tongue tip touching the teeth. It is used preceding forward vowels and diphthongs. Read aloud these words and feel the placement of the tip of your tongue touching the teeth: *leap, lit, let, lot, late.* The IPA symbol for this clear sound is [l̟].

Next, there is the dark [l], sometimes called the alveolar [l]. The tip of the tongue touches higher up on the teeth ridge. Generally, Americans use the dark [l] at the ends of words or in the middle of words. Feel the placement of the tip of your tongue against the teeth ridge as you read these words: *full, help, wall, fell, challenge, inland, truly.* The IPA symbol for this dark sound is [ɫ].

In English there is a dental [l] which Americans use preceding *th.* Feel the tip of the tongue on or between your teeth as you read these words: *wealth, stealth, health. Sell the car. Will they go?* This sound is represented in IPA by [l̪]. Dental [l̪] becomes a distortion called tongue thrust when it is used consistently for [l] in English in words other than before *th.*

The clear [l̟] and dental [l̪] are often used in foreign languages, while the dark [ɫ] is neither common nor desirable in other languages. American singers will need to identify and use the clear [l̟] or dental [l̪] for singing in Italian, German and French.

This manual will simply use the unmodified symbol [l] unless there is a need to indicate one of the allophones listed above.

Lastly, in words like *little, bottle,* or *able,* the final *le* is spoken as a *vowelized* or *syllabized l.* The IPA transcription for this fourth allophone uses a dot underneath the symbol [l̩]. In singing, however, the *syllabic l* [l̩] does not produce a freely vibrating tone on sustained notes. Therefore, singers sing on the vowel [ə] followed by an [l]. *Syllabic l* [l̩] will be transcribed as [əl] in this text.

Word	Spoken	Sung
little	[ˈlɪ tl̩]	[ˈlɪ təl]
bottle	[ˈbɑ tl̩]	[ˈbɑ təl]
able	[ˈeɪ bl̩]	[ˈeɪ bəl]

A. Articulation drills for [l].

Read aloud these sounds. Practice this drill using a clear [l̟] and a dropped jaw. Give attention to the flexible lifting of the tip of the tongue to the back of the teeth to produce the clear [l̟].

[l̟a l̟a l̟a]   [l̟oʊ l̟oʊ l̟oʊ]   [l̟u l̟u l̟u]   [l̟a l̟a l̟a]

Read aloud these words using a dark [ɫ]. Be sure that your tongue tip firmly touches the teeth ridge for each [ɫ].

wall

elevate

relevant

alright

help

only

told

Read aloud these words, noticing that the *l* is silent. Be sure you do not pronounce the *l* in these words.

walk	psalm
balk	alms
talk	calf
calm	half

B. Transcribe into IPA symbols these words using [l] .

Read aloud the words as you write, articulating [l] clearly and easily.

Initial

1. lit   [ɫɪt]   4. limb _____

2. leap _____   5. leaf _____

3. lose _____   6. liver _____

Medial

1. wealthy _____   4. delicate _____

2. pulpit _____   5. shoulder _____

3. sulky _____   6. selling _____

Final

1. funnel _____   4. purple _____

2. middle _____   5. cattle _____

3. recall _____   6. opal _____

C. Transcribe these IPA symbols into English words.

1. ['mɪ lər] _____   6. [vaɪl] _____

2. [ɔl] _____   7. ['si lɪŋ] _____

3. ['seɪ lər] _____   8. [leɪm] _____

4. [ɔl 'rɛ dɪ] _____   9. [lɪd] _____

5. ['kæ lən dər] _____   10. [boʊl] _____

D. Vocalize with [l].

[la   la   la   la   la   la   la   la   la]

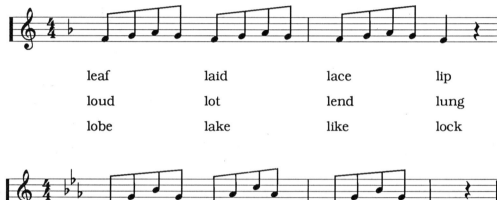

leaf	laid	lace	lip
loud	lot	lend	lung
lobe	lake	like	lock

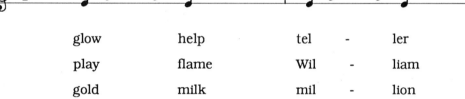

glow	help	tel	-	ler
play	flame	Wil	-	liam
gold	milk	mil	-	lion

ap - ple, rat - tle   a - ble   hill_____

mid - dle   o - pal   pur - ple   wall_____

E. Sentences with [l].

Read aloud these sentences, articulating the [l] clearly and easily.

Luckily, little lads love long-limbed lasses.

Alright! All the old cold milk has been sold!

Chapter 12 Worksheet

Transcribe these words into IPA symbols.

1. left	_____	11. latter	_____
2. hall	_____	12. ruling	_____
3. elbow	_____	13. lather	_____
4. olfactory	_____	14. fallable	_____
5. lace	_____	15. abdominal	_____
6. locust	_____	16. intercostal	_____
7. elevate	_____	17. loudly	_____
8. feelings	_____	18. loathe	_____
9. roller	_____	19. choral	_____
10. liquid	_____	20. cerebral	_____

Transcribe these IPA symbols into English words.

1. [ˈʌn dər ˌlaɪ ɪŋ]	_____	6. [ˈsoʊ ˌloʊ ɪst]	_____
2. [ˈli dər]	_____	7. [ˈfɑ ˌloʊd]	_____
3. [ˈbæ ləns]	_____	8. [ˈteɪ lər]	_____
4. [ˈpis miəl]	_____	9. [ˈmɑ nə ˌlɔg]	_____
5. [ˈmæ lɪt]	_____	10. [ɪn ˈteɪl]	_____

Chapter 13
The
Glides

A glide is a consonant whose sound is characterized by a movement of the articulators from one position to another. Glides are sometimes referred to as semi-vowels or semi-consonants.

The glides in English are:

The *r* glide [**r**], as in <u>r</u>ose, <u>r</u>ed, <u>r</u>am.

The *y* glide [**j**], called *yot* [**jɔt**], as in <u>y</u>es, <u>y</u>ou, <u>y</u>esterday.

The *w* glides, voiced [**w**] as in <u>w</u>ere and unvoiced [**hw**] as in <u>wh</u>en.

[r] [j] [hw] [w]

Exercises

The glide [r]

Description

IPA Symbol	[r]
Word Example	*rose* *price* *berry*
Voicing	voiced
Place of Articulation	tongue tip just back of teeth ridge
Manner of Articulation	glide The vocal folds vibrate as the sides of the tongue press against the inside of the upper back teeth. The tongue tip is retracted and pointed upward just behind the teeth ridge. The soft palate is raised, closing the nasal passageway.

Common Problems

Excessive retraction of the tip of the tongue.

The addition of [r] where it should not exist: *idear, Louisianar, warsh.*

The rounding of the lips when forming an [r], which results in a sound similar to [w]. *Red* should not sound like *wed.*

The consonant [r] is classified as a glide because it is produced with a continuous movement of the tongue from one position to another. Notice the gliding movement of the tongue as you say the words *red, rose, drip,* and *trip.*

When *r* follows a vowel in the same syllable, it can sometimes be heard as a separate consonant as in *car* or as part of the vowels [ɝ] and [ɚ] as in m<u>ur</u>d<u>er</u>.

You will need to listen to your own speech to determine whether *r* is part of a vowel sound, or whether it is separate from the vowel. Read Chapter 6, Central Vowels, for information about transcribing and singing the r-colored vowels.

The *rolled r* [r̃] is used in other languages but is not usually spoken in English. However, it is occasionally used in singing when a stronger articulation is needed, as with an orchestra in a large hall. Vocalizing on the *rolled r* [r̃] is also a valuable exercise to achieve greater tongue flexibility.

A *one-tap r* [ɾ], as in the British pronunciation of *ve<u>r</u>y*, is also used occasionally by singers for additional clarity to communicate the word.

A. Articulation drills for [r].

Read these words aloud giving attention to your articulation of [r].

<u>r</u>ose	be<u>r</u>ate	bee<u>r</u>
<u>r</u>ed	e<u>r</u>ode	wi<u>r</u>e
<u>r</u>ace	p<u>r</u>etend	chai<u>r</u>
<u>r</u>an	f<u>r</u>iend	dea<u>r</u>
w<u>r</u>ong	b<u>r</u>ing	he<u>r</u>e
w<u>r</u>ap	c<u>r</u>amp	sta<u>r</u>
<u>r</u>est	g<u>r</u>ew	you<u>r</u>
<u>r</u>etrieved	app<u>r</u>oach	hai<u>r</u>
<u>r</u>easonable	t<u>r</u>ack	sta<u>r</u>e

Read aloud these words to contrast [r] and [w]. Do not use excessive lip movement. Feel the movement of the tongue on [r].

reed	weed
red	wed
rate	wait
ride	wide
rays	ways

B. Transcribe these words into IPA symbols.

Initial

1. rose   [roʊz]   5. wrecked _____

2. red   _____   6. right   _____

3. rail   _____   7. raw   _____

4. reel   _____   8. rate   _____

Medial

1. aground _____   5. arrest   _____

2. erode   _____   6. trite   _____

3. very   _____   7. three   _____

4. uproot _____   8. awry   _____

Final

1. car   _____   5. fore   _____

2. fear   _____   6. pear   _____

3. par   _____   7. pair   _____

4. tour   _____   8. dear   _____

C. Transcribe these IPA symbols into English words.

1. ['ri zən] _____   6. ['fju rɪ əs] _____

2. [rif]   _____   7. ['kæ rɪ] _____

3. [frɛnd] _____   8. ['fri lɪ] _____

4. [brɪŋ] _____   9. [raɪts] _____

5. ['mɪ stə rɪ] _____   10. [moʊr] _____

D. Vocalize with [r].

trilled [r̝]: r r r r r r r r r r r r r r r r r r r r r

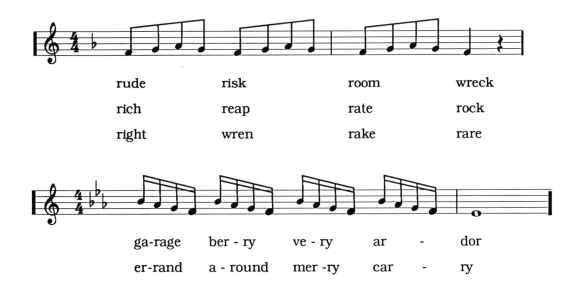

rude	risk	room	wreck
rich	reap	rate	rock
right	wren	rake	rare

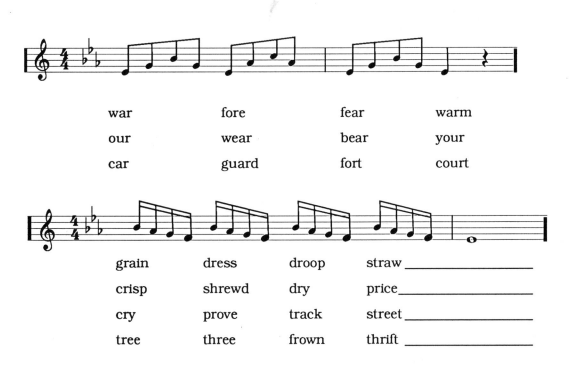

| ga-rage | ber - ry | ve - ry | ar - dor |
| er-rand | a - round | mer -ry | car - ry |

war	fore	fear	warm
our	wear	bear	your
car	guard	fort	court

grain	dress	droop	straw _____
crisp	shrewd	dry	price_____
cry	prove	track	street_____
tree	three	frown	thrift _____

E. Sentence with [r].

Read aloud, articulating the [r] sound clearly and easily.

Ruby rode Ralph's rich, red roan rapidly.

Exercises

The y glide [j], as in *yes* [jɛs]

The symbol [j] is called *yot* [j]

Description

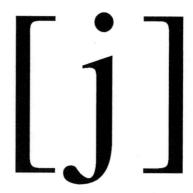

IPA Symbol	[j]
Word Example	*yes* *million*
Voicing	voiced
Place of Articulation	tongue and hard palate
Manner of Articulation	glide The tongue tip touches the back of the bottom front teeth. The blade of the tongue moves to a high, arched position, close to the hard palate, similar to the vowel [ɪ], then quickly shifts to the vowel which follows. The soft palate is raised.

Common Problems

The substitution of [ʤ] for [j]. *Did you?* becomes *Did jew?*

The addition of [j] between words which end and begin with a vowel. *I am* becomes *I yam.*

A. Articulation drills for [j].

Read aloud the following words with an initial *jot* [j].

ye

year

you

yes

Read aloud these words which include [j] after [l] and [n].

million	['mɪl jən]
stallion	['stæl jən]
billiards	['bɪl jərdz]
onion	['ʌn jən]
opinion	[ə 'pɪn jən]
companion	[cəm 'pæn jən]

Read aloud these phrases. Do not add a [j] sound between words which end and begin with a vowel sound.

I am	not	I yam
see it	not	see yit
joy in	not	joy yin

Read aloud these words, carefully articulating the [j] sound.

Would you?	not	Would djew?
I'll let you.	not	I'll let chew.
Beside you.	not	Beside djew.

Read aloud the following paired words to contrast the sound of pure [u] and diphthongal [ju]. See Chapter 7 for a discussion of [ju].

[u]		[ju]	
food	[fud]	feud	[fjud]
coo	[ku]	cue	[cju]
booze	[buz]	abuse	[ə 'bjuz]
booty	['bu tɪ]	beauty	['bju tɪ]

Read aloud these words which use [j].

uniform	['ju nə ˌfɔrm]
ewe	[ju]
usual	['ju ʒʊ əl]

B. Transcribe these words into IPA symbols.

Initial

1. yield [jild]   4. unified _____

2. yam _____   5. usage _____

3. youth _____   6. yesterday _____

Medial

1. pinion _____   4. civilian _____

2. union _____   5. canyon _____

3. billion _____   6. William _____

Final

There are no final [j] sounds in English.

C. Transcribe these IPA symbols into English words.

1. ['trɪl jən] _____   5. ['jou ga] _____

2. [jɛt] _____   6 [jæŋk] _____

3. ['jɛ lo] _____   7. [jist] _____

4. ['ju nɪt] _____   8. [jɪr] _____

D. Vocalize, carefully articulating each [j].

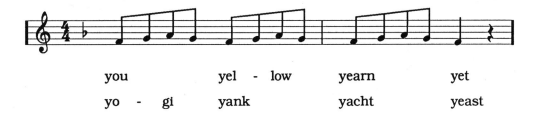

you   yel - low   yearn   yet

yo - gi   yank   yacht   yeast

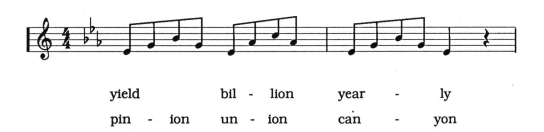

yield   bil - lion   year - ly

pin - ion   un - ion   can - yon

E. Sentence with [j].

Read aloud, articulating each [j] clearly and easily.

Yards yield yellow yams yearly.

Exercises

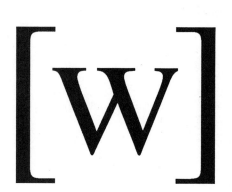

The w glides [hw] and [w]
The symbol [hw] is called
unvoiced w
The symbol [w] is called "w"

Description

IPA Symbol	**[hw]**	**[w]**
Word Example	*when*	*went*
Voicing	unvoiced	voiced
Place of Articulation	both lips	
Manner of Articulation	glide The tongue tip is behind the back of the bottom front teeth. The back of the tongue is raised. The lips are rounded and ready to move into the next sound. The soft palate is raised, closing off the nasal passageway.	

Common Problems

The substitution of voiced **[w]** for unvoiced **[hw]**. *Whine* **[hwaɪn]** should not sound like *wine* **[waɪn]**.

Inadequate lip rounding for **[hw]** and **[w]**.

A. Articulation drills for unvoiced w [hw] and voiced w [w].

Place your hand on the front of your throat, on the Adam's apple, and say the following sounds. Feel the vibration that occurs for [w] but not for [hw].

Read aloud the following sounds to contrast the voiced and unvoiced qualities of [w] and [hw].

[w]   [hw]   [w]   [hw]   [w]   [hw]

Be sure to use adequate lip rounding for these sounds.

Most speakers of standard American English use the unvoiced w [hw] for the *wh* in such words as <u>wheel</u>, <u>where</u>, and <u>what</u>. However, using unvoiced w [hw] seems to be declining in certain parts of the United States. As you will see in the following list of paired words, the use of unvoiced w [hw] and voiced w [w] helps distinguish meanings. Therefore, in singing, you should continue to use [hw] for the *wh* words.

Read aloud these paired words to contrast the sounds of unvoiced w [hw] and voiced [w]. Do you use [hw] in your dialect?

Another IPA symbol which is sometimes used for voiceless [hw] is [ʍ].

[hw]	[w]
wheel	weal
whine	wine
whey	way
where	wear
which	witch
whether	weather

Read aloud these words which use the [h] sound.

who	[hu]
whose	[huz]
whom	[hum]
whole	[houl]
whore	[hour]

*There are some words beginning with the spelling **wh** in which the initial sound is not the unvoiced w [hw] but is simply [h].*

Read aloud these words in which the *w* is silent.

written	['rɪ tən]
wracked	[rækt]
wren	[rɛn]
wring	[rɪŋ]
wrinkle	['rɪŋ kəl]

*Words beginning with **wr** are pronounced with [r] only, the letter **w** being silent.*

B. Transcribe these words into IPA symbols. The words use both unvoiced [hw] and voiced [w].

Read aloud these paired words as you write the IPA transcription to contrast **[hw]** and **[w]**.

	[hw]		[w]
1. whirled	[hwɜrld]	world	[wɜrld]
2. whale	_____	wail	_____
3. whither	_____	wither	_____
4. wheat	_____	we	_____
5. while	_____	wile	_____
6. whirred	_____	word	_____
7. whine	_____	wine	_____
8. whisper	_____	wisp	_____
9. whet	_____	wet	_____
10. white	_____	wild	_____

Read aloud these words that contain a **[w]** sound following another consonant. Write the transcription.

1. swag	_____	5. quit	_____
2. dwell	_____	6. quail	_____
3. twenty	_____	7. quick	_____
4. dwarf	_____	8. choir	_____

C. Transcribe these IPA symbols into English words.

1. [hweɪl]	_____	6. [kweɪl]	_____
2. [weɪ]	_____	7. ['swɑ lo]	_____
3. ['hwɪ səl]	_____	8. ['wɔl nət]	_____
4. [waɪn]	_____	9. [hwɜrl]	_____
5. [kwɪl]	_____	10. [wɜr]	_____

D. Vocalize, articulating the unvoiced [hw] and voiced [w] sounds carefully.

why	white	what_____
wine	weak	wise _____
whirled	world	won _____

E. Sentences with [hw] and [w].

Read these sentences aloud, articulating each unvoiced *w* [hw] and voiced *w* [w] clearly and easily.

Why whisper for whiskey and whine for wheat?

Whirl and whip the white whey.

Watch out! The wicked woman wants Wilma's water well.

Wise witches won't wear wool.

Chapter 13 Worksheet

Transcribe these words into IPA symbols.

1. worthy	_____	11. wring	_____
2. whiskers	_____	12. yammer	_____
3. razed	_____	13. whirl	_____
4. unwieldy	_____	14. punitive	_____
5. cupid	_____	15. while	_____
6. arrest	_____	16. unique	_____
7. wander	_____	17. wise	_____
8. yearly	_____	18. tweet	_____
9. wry	_____	19. whatever	_____
10. ukulele	_____	20. valued	_____

Transcribe these IPA symbols into English words.

1. [twɪst]	_____	6. [hwɪz]	_____
2. [hwɔrf]	_____	7. [twikt]	_____
3. [wɪŋk]	_____	8. [rɔŋ]	_____
4. ['pju mə]	_____	9. ['wɑm ˌbæt]	_____
5. ['stju pər]	_____	10. [kruz]	_____

CHAPTER 14
THE
COMBINATION
CONSONANTS

The combination consonants, also called affricatives, are those which combine the articulation of two consonant sounds into a single speech unit. In English, there are two combination consonants, both of which are composed of a stop-plosive and a fricative consonant. The combination consonants are:

The cognates [ʧ] as in <u>ch</u>eek and [ʤ] as in <u>j</u>eer or <u>g</u>in.

[ʧ]   [ʤ]

Exercises

The combination consonants [ʧ] and [ʤ]

Description

[ʧ]

[ʤ]

IPA Symbol	[ʧ]	[ʤ]
Word Example	*chill*	*jet* *gin*
Voicing	unvoiced	voiced
Place of Articulation	tongue and boundary of teeth ridge and hard palate	
Manner of Articulation	combination The tongue blade touches the teeth ridge and the sides of the tongue touch the upper side teeth to form a stop-plosive sound. The tongue tip then moves to a fricative position. The soft palate is raised closing off the nasal passageway.	

The consonants [ʧ] and [ʤ] are called by their sound.

Common Problems

Lisping air escapes laterally, out of the sides of the mouth.

A. Articulation drills for [ʧ] and [ʤ].

Place your hand on the front of your throat, on the Adam's apple, and say the following sounds. Feel the vibration that occurs for [ʤ] but not for [ʧ].

Articulate each [ʧ] and [ʤ] with precision, giving attention to the voicing and the manner of articulation (stop-plosive followed by fricative).

Read aloud the following sounds in isolation to contrast the unvoiced [ʧ] and voiced [ʤ].

[ʧ] [ʤ]   [ʧ ʧ] [ʤ ʤ]   [ʧ] [ʤ]

Read aloud the following words to contrast [ʧ] and [ʤ].

unvoiced [ʧ]	voiced [ʤ]
chose	jewel
champ	jam
China	angina
child	Giles
breech	bridge
match	Madge

Read aloud these words to contrast [ʧ] and [ʤ] with other voiced and unvoiced sounds.

[s]	[ʃ]	[ʧ]
sea	she	cheep
sop	shop	chop
bass	bash	batch
distant	dishes	ditches

[z]	[ʒ]	[ʤ]
zeal	adhesion	Jean
zip	visionary	gyp
has	azure	Madge
busy	collision	pidgeon

Read aloud to contrast [ʃ] and [ʧ].

[ʃ]	[ʧ]
share	chair
she	cheap
ship	chip
marsh	march
hush	hutch
cash	catch
luscious	lunch

Read aloud to contrast [ʒ] and [ʤ].

[ʒ]	[ʤ]
beige	hedge
casual	surging
fusion	fudge
leisure	legion
mirage	smudge

B. Transcribe these words into IPA symbols.

Read aloud the words as you write the symbols, articulating each [ʧ] and [ʤ] clearly and easily.

Initial

1. chill   [tʃɪl]   6. gentle _____
2. Jill   [dʒɪl]   7. chump _____
3. chest _____   8. jump _____
4. jest _____   9. cheap _____
5. chin _____   10. Gene _____

Medial

1. etching _____   6. regent _____
2. edging _____   7. lunches _____
3. searching _____   8. lunges _____
4. surging _____   9. ketchup _____
5. richest _____   10. midget _____

Final

1. leech _____   6. grudge _____
2. ledge _____   7. crutch _____
3. perch _____   8. strange _____
4. purge _____   9. church _____
5. hatch _____   10. judge _____

C. Transcribe these IPA symbols into English words.

1. ['ʧɪl drɪn] _____   6. [ʤus] _____
2. [ʤɛm] _____   7. ['hæ ʧɪt] _____
3. [səg 'ʤɛst] _____   8. [ʤeɪl] _____
4. ['rɪ ʧʊ əl] _____   9. ['pɜr ʤʊ rɪ] _____
5. ['ʧɛ lɪst] _____   10. ['vɜr ʧu] _____

D. Vocalize, using [tʃ] and [dʒ].

chip	Jean	cheese _____
Chad	Jane	cheap _____
chump	jest	chest _____

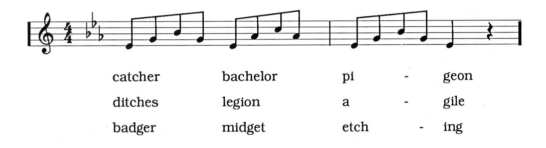

catcher	bachelor	pi	-	geon
ditches	legion	a	-	gile
badger	midget	etch	-	ing

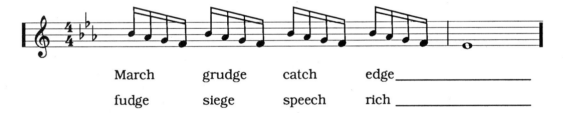

| March | grudge | catch | edge _____ |
| fudge | siege | speech | rich _____ |

E. Sentences with [tʃ] and [dʒ].

Read aloud the following sentences, articulating each [tʃ] and [dʒ] clearly and easily.

Charlie's chilly children chase Chet's chickens.

Jeff just joined Judd's jazzy jiggers.

Chapter 14 Worksheet

Transcribe these words into IPA symbols.

1. virtuous	_____	16. Butch	_____
2. cheese	_____	17. gouge	_____
3. natural	_____	18. picture	_____
4. larger	_____	19. such	_____
5. lodge	_____	20. surge	_____
6. coach	_____	21. jump	_____
7. watcher	_____	22. gentle	_____
8. peach	_____	23. chum	_____
9. huge	_____	24. joke	_____
10. choke	_____	25. agent	_____
11. match	_____	26. choice	_____
12. damage	_____	27. juice	_____
13. structure	_____	28. soldier	_____
14. wage	_____	29. itch	_____
15. pouch	_____	30. page	_____

Transcribe these IPA symbols into English words.

1. [bʌʤ]	_____	11. [stɪʧ]	_____
2. [hɛʤ]	_____	12. [səg ˈʤɛs ʧən]	_____
3. [ˈpɪ ʤən]	_____	13. [ʧɪn]	_____
4. [mʌʧ]	_____	14. [kauʧ]	_____
5. [ʧif]	_____	15. [ʧɔk]	_____
6. [ˈkwɛs ʧən]	_____	16. [ˈfɜr nɪ ʧər]	_____
7. [ˈfju ʧər]	_____	17. [riʧ]	_____
8. [ˈmɜr ʤər]	_____	18. [ʧeɪn]	_____
9. [ə ˈʤɛn də]	_____	19. [ʤɔɪ]	_____
10. [ʤɑr]	_____	20. [ˈʤɛ nə rəl]	_____

CHAPTER 15
ADDITIONAL
IPA SYMBOLS
FOR ITALIAN
FRENCH
AND GERMAN

Phonemes and Allophones in Foreign Languages

Each language has its own patterns for articulating individual speech sounds. The way a vowel is spoken in English may have variations in other languages. In French, for example, the phoneme [e] is articulated with the high point of the tongue closer to the roof of the mouth than in English, so close, in fact, that it sounds almost like an [i] to many Americans. The close, forward French [e], therefore, is an allophone of the phoneme [e].

The French *schwa* [ə] also has a different sound from the *schwa* in English. The English *schwa* [ə] is a weakened mid-central *uh* [ʌ] sound. But the French *schwa* [ə] is a more forward and rounded sound. It can be considered the unstressed counterpart of the mixed vowel [ø]. American singers must be very careful about the articulation of the French *schwa* [ə].

Other IPA phonemes which have allophones in other languages include the [t], [d] and [n] consonants which are articulated in English with the tongue tip at the teeth ridge. In foreign languages, these consonants become dental, with the tongue tip touching the teeth instead of the teeth ridge.

Mixed Vowels

There will be many sounds to be considered as you learn the pronunciation rules of a new language and your diction teacher will instruct you in the particular sounds of each language. This chapter will be devoted solely to the presentation of additional IPA symbols which are used in Italian, German and French, but not in English.

Mixed Vowels

The mixed vowels are those vowels articulated with the tongue in a high, forward position as for a forward vowel, while the lips are rounded, as for a back vowel. For example, put your tongue in the position for *ee* [i] and then, *without moving the tongue*, round your lips and say *ōo* [u]. The resulting sound will be the close mixed vowel [y], a blending of the two sounds [i] and [u]. Although mixed vowels are not found in English, they are used in both German and French.

When reading IPA transcriptions aloud, mixed vowels can be referred to in three ways. The most common way is simply to call them by their sound. A second way of referring to them labels their overall method of production (from the most close to most open) by calling them *first position* [y], *second position* [ʏ], *third position* [ø], and *fourth position* [œ]. Naming the vowel in this manner can help clarify communication about the vowel sound in a class situation when the articulation of each mixed vowel sound may not yet be totally accurate.

There is a third way to refer to the mixed vowels. In the German language, mixed vowels are written with an *umlaut* (two small dots) over the letters *ü* or *ö*, as in the words, *früh* and *schön*. The vowels are referred to as *close* and *open umlauted ü*, [y] and [ʏ], designating the fact that the space in the mouth for the first vowel is more close than for the second, and *close* and *open umlauted ö*, [ø] and [œ], which again designates the relative close and open spacial relationship of the two sounds. These Germanic names are often used for the mixed vowels in diction classes and are useful for communication. You may choose which of the three methods of naming mixed vowels you wish to use.

Description of Mixed Vowels

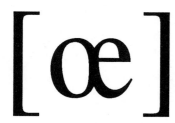

There are four mixed vowel sounds represented by the IPA symbols [y], [ʏ], [ø], [œ]. These sounds are produced with the tongue and lips in the positions indicated on the following chart. For each mixed vowel, start with the high, forward tongue position suggested ([i], [ɪ], [e], or [ɛ]). Then, *without moving the tongue*, say the second vowel which uses the rounded lips of the back vowels [u], [ʊ], [o], or [ɔ]).

It must be pointed out that to produce the mixed vowel the speaker does not glide from the forward vowel to the back vowel. Instead, both vowels are produced *simultaneously*. It is the combining of the two sounds into a unified single vowel sound that results in the mixed vowel.

Chart of Tongue and Lip positions for the Mixed Vowels

	Tongue position		Lip position		Resulting mixed vowel
1.	[i]	+	[u]	=	[y]
2	[ɪ]	+	[ʊ]	=	[ʏ]
3.	[e]	+	[o]	=	[ø]
4.	[ɛ]	+	[ɔ]	=	[œ]

A. Practice the mixed vowels [y ʏ ø œ].

Practice these sounds repeatedly until you can articulate them easily and accurately. These are new sounds to most Americans and you may need some extra guidance from someone who knows these vowel sounds well. When saying these vowels, be very specific about how they feel and sound in order to learn them accurately.

Look in a mirror as you practice to see the position of your jaw, lips, and tongue. Whisper the vowels in the following order and watch for the rounding of your lips and the high, forward position of the tongue for each of the vowels. The jaw, lips, and tongue move progressively from a more close position to a more open position as you *whisper* this list of mixed vowels.

1. [y] (tongue as [i] and lips as [u])

2. [ʏ] (tongue as [ɪ] and lips as [ʊ])

3. [ø] (tongue as [e] and lips as [o])

4. [œ] (tongue as [ɛ] and lips as [ɔ])

Whisper, then speak each of the vowels using a normal conversational voice.

1. Whisper [y], speak [y].

2. Whisper [ʏ], speak [ʏ].

3. Whisper [ø], speak [ø].

4. Whisper [œ], speak [œ].

After speaking the vowels in the order suggested, reverse the order, going from the most open mixed vowel, *fourth position* [œ], to the most close mixed vowel, *first position* [y].

[œ]

[ø]

[ʏ]

[y]

B. Practice these German words which use mixed vowels.

Read aloud these words using *close umlaut ü* [y].

für	[fyː r]
glüht	[glyː t]
süss	[zyː s]
lügen	[lyː gən]
Frühling	[fryː lɪŋ]
müde	[myː də]
blüht	[blyː t]
über	[yː bər]

The IPA symbol [ː] indicates that the preceding sound should be prolonged.

Read aloud these words using open umlaut ü [ʏ].

müsst	[mʏsː st]
zurück	[tsu ˈrʏk]
Glück	[glʏk]
gebückt	[gəˈbʏkt]
Sünde	[ˈzʏn də]
Künste	[ˈkʏn stə]
Mütter	[ˈmʏtː tər]

Read aloud these words using *close umlaut ö* [ø].

hört	[hørt]
Söhnen	[ˈzø nən]
lösen	[ˈlø zən]
böse	[ˈbø zə]
dösen	[ˈdø zən]
löhne	[ˈlø nə]
Öhren	[ˈø rən]
schön	[ʃøn]

Read aloud these words using *open umlaut o* [œ]

Hölle	['hœlː lə]
könnte	['kœn tə]
Götter	['gœtː tər]
Mörder	['mœr dər]
löscht	[lœʃt]
gönnte	['gœn tə]
zwölf	[tsvœlf]
öffen	['œfːfnən]

C. Practice these French words using [y ø œ]. The second position [ʏ] vowel sound is not used in the French language.

Read aloud these words using [y].

tu	[ty]
sur	[syr]
Luxe	[lyksə]
du	[dy]
lune	[ly nə]
sud	[syd]
muter	[my te]
pure	[py rə]

Read aloud these words using [ø].

feu	[fø]
deux	[dø]
bleu	[blø]
yeux	[jø]
cieux	[sjø]
pleut	[plø]
jeu	[ʒø]
fameux	[fa mø]

Read aloud these words using [œ].

seul	[sœl]
coeur	[kœr]
meurt	[mœr]
boeuf	[bœf]
jeune	[ʒœ nə]
soeur	[sœr]
pleurer	[plœ re]
douceur	[du sœr]

French Nasal Vowels

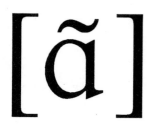

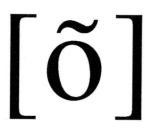

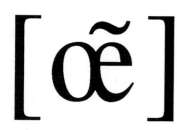

The French Nasal Vowels

The four nasal vowels in French [ɛ̃], [ɑ̃], [õ], and [œ̃], are produced by slightly lowering the soft palate and permitting air to enter the nose. It is important that the nasal vowels do not become so nasal as to be sharply twangy in quality. Listen to French singers and you will hear how beautifully these vowel sounds can be sung. In fact, many voice teachers recommend the use of nasal vowels to help women achieve head voice or men achieve the covered tone.

The nasal vowel sound is formed by the combination of the vowel plus the nasal consonant. In the word *son* [sõ], the letters *on* form a unit and are pronounced as [õ]. The *n* is not pronounced, it is silent. A listing of the four French nasal vowels follows.

The nasal vowel [ɛ̃] is nasalized [ɛ]. It is used in words like *bien* [bjɛ̃], *matin* [ma tɛ̃] and *simple* [sɛ̃ plə].

The nasal vowel [ɑ̃] is nasalized [ɑ]. It is used in words like *champ* [ʃɑ̃], *enfant* [ɑ̃ fɑ̃], and *dans* [dɑ̃].

The nasal vowel [õ] is nasalized [o]. It is used in words like *son* [sõ], *bon* [bõ], and *tombeau* [tõ bo].

The nasal vowel [œ̃] is nasalized [œ]. It is used in words like *parfum* [par fœ̃], *un* [œ̃], and *humble* [œ̃ blə].

Language is constantly changing and variations within languages will occur. This is true of the sounds of the French nasals [ɑ̃] and [õ].

Although the IPA symbol [ɑ̃] represents the nasalized [ɑ], pure [ɑ] is pronounced with unrounded lips, while the nasal [ɑ̃] is pronounced with slightly rounded lips, resulting in a vowel which sounds almost like [ɔ̃]. This sound may be considered an allophone of [ɑ̃]. Read these words aloud and feel the slight rounding of your lips which occurs on [ɑ̃]. *Vent* [vɑ̃], *temps* [tɑ̃], *quand* [kɑ̃].

The second nasal vowel which needs clarification is [õ].

---

*In French, a vowel is nasalized when it precedes a final **m** or **n** or precedes an **m** or **n** which is followed by another consonant other than **m** or **n**.*

*In liaison, which is the connecting of a final consonant to the initial vowel sound of the next word, **m** and **n** are pronounced.*

In IPA, a tilde [˜] indicates the vowel is nasalized. For example, [ɛ̃] would be a nasalized [ɛ].

Until recently, dictionaries and texts have transcribed the vowel [õ] as [ɔ̃]. Yet, the sound of [ɔ̃] is really too open for this French nasal vowel and can be easily confused with the slightly rounded allophone of [ɑ̃]. Read these words aloud, using the well rounded lips of [õ]. *Ont* [õ], *leçons* [lə sõ], *sombre* [sõ brə].

A. Practice the French nasal vowels.

Read aloud these words with the nasal vowel [ɛ̃].

jardin	[ʒar dɛ̃]	loin	[lwɛ̃]
importe	[ɛ̃ pɔr tə]	ainsi	[ɛ̃ si]
reviens	[rə vjɛ̃]	main	[mɛ̃]
pleins	[plɛ̃]	insulte	[ɛ̃ syl tə]
chemin	[ʃə mɛ̃]	vainqueur	[vɛ̃ kœr]

In spoken French, the final schwa [ə] is silent. In singing, when the final schwa [ə] is given a note, it is pronounced.

Read aloud these words with the nasal vowel [ɑ̃].

entends	[ɑ̃ tɑ̃]	dimanche	[di mɑ̃ ʃə]
quand	[kɑ̃]	sentier	[sɑ̃ tje]
temps	[tɑ̃]	encore	[ɑ̃ kɔ rə]
prends	[prɑ̃]	chante	[ʃɑ̃ tə]
sembler	[sɑ̃ ble]	pamphlet	[pɑ̃ flɛ]

Read aloud these words with the nasal vowel [õ].

ton	[tõ]	sont	[sõ]
maison	[mɛ zõ]	long	[lõ]
songe	[sõ ʒə]	horizon	[o ri zõ]
tombe	[tõ bə]	ombre	[õ brə]
front	[frõ]	papillons	[pa pi jõ]

Read aloud these words with the nasal vowel [œ̃].

défunts	[de fœ̃]
humble	[œ̃ blə]
un	[œ̃]
parfum	[par fœ̃]

Italian and French *enya*

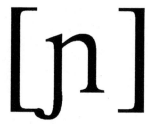

The Italian and French *enya* [ɲ]

The IPA symbol [ɲ], called *enya*, represents the *gn* sound in Italian, as in *ogni*, and in French, as in *digne*. In English, the closest sound which can be found to the Italian and French *enya* [ɲ] is the [nj] in the word *onion* ['ʌ njən]. The [nj] in *onion*, however, requires the tip of the tongue to lift to the teeth ridge for [n] then lower to the back of the bottom front teeth for [j]. The *enya* [ŋ], by contrast, is produced with a single tongue action.

To produce *enya* [ɲ], slightly part your lips, put the tip of the tongue behind the bottom front teeth and lift the blade of the tongue to touch the front of the hard palate. Add voice, and you will be producing the nasal, palatal consonant sound *enya* [ɲ]. The sound is something like an [n], except that it is made with the *blade* of the tongue touching the *palate* rather than the *tip* of the tongue touching the teeth *ridge.*

A. Practice the *enya* [ɲ].

Sing, humming with the nasal consonants [n] and [ɲ].

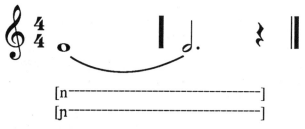

Sing, sustaining [n] and [ɲ] and the following vowels.
Feel the movement of the tongue tip as it lifts to touch the teeth ridge for [n], then lowers for the vowel [i].

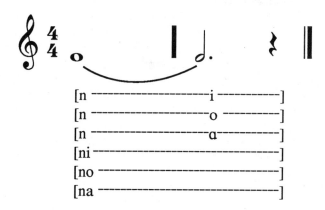

Feel the contact of the blade of the tongue with the hard palate for [ɲ]. The tip of the tongue remains behind the bottom front teeth to produce both the *enya* [ɲ] and the vowel [i].

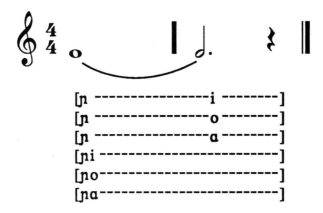

[ɲ --------------- i -------]
[ɲ --------------- o -------]
[ɲ --------------- a -------]
[ɲi -----------------------]
[ɲo-----------------------]
[ɲa-----------------------]

Read aloud these Italian words using [ɲ].

degno	['de ɲɔ]	bisogna	[bi 'zo ɲa]
segno	['se ɲɔ]	Signori	[si ɲo ri]
compagno	[kom 'pa ɲɔ]	sognare	[so ɲa rɛ]
cognome	['ko ɲo mɛ]	regno	['re ɲɔ]

Read aloud these French words using [ɲ].

agneau	[a ɲo]	peignoir	[pɛ ɲwar]
magnifique	[ma ɲi fik]	dignite	[di ɲi tɛ]
peigne	[pɛ ɲə]	dignes	[di ɲə]
vignes	[vi ɲə]	bagne	[ba ɲə]

The
Italian
elya

The Italian *Elya* [ʎ]

Elya [ʎ] is a lateral, non-fricative, palatal consonant which is used in Italian in e*gli* and vo*gliamo*. In Italian, *elya* [ʎ] is spelled *gli*.

In English, the closest sound to *elya* [ʎ] is in mi*lli*on ['mɪl jən]. The [lj] in *million*, however, the tip of the tongue touches the teeth ridge for the consonant [l] and then moves to the back of the bottom front teeth for the glide [j]. The *elya* [ʎ], by contrast, is produced with a single tongue action.

To produce *elya* [ʎ], slightly part your lips, put the tip of your tongue behind the bottom front teeth, arch the front of your tongue, lifting it to touch the front of the hard palate. Add voice and let the air exit laterally over the sides of the tongue. The sound will be something like an [l], only it is made with the *blade* of the tongue, not the tip, against the boundary between the teeth ridge and the hard palate.

A. Practice the Italian *elya* [ʎ].

Sing these sounds, leaving the tongue tip behind the back of the bottom front teeth for both the [ʎ] and the vowel which follows. Feel the movement in the body of the tongue as you go from the consonant [y] to the vowel.

```
[ʎi -------------------------]
[ʎɛ -------------------------]
[ʎɑ -------------------------]
[ʎɔ -------------------------]
[ʎu -------------------------]
```

Read aloud these Italian words using [ʎ].

egli	['e ʎi]
gli	[ʎi]
foglia	['fɔ ʎɑ]
Pagliacci	[pɑ 'ʎɑtː ʧi]
voglia	['vo ʎa]
figlio	['fi ʎɔ]
Guglielmo	[gu 'ʎɛl mɔ]
consiglio	[kon 'si ʎɔ]

The French Glide [ɥ]

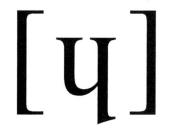

The IPA symbol [ɥ] is a shortened form of the mixed vowel [y], and is referred to by its sound. The [ɥ], along with [w] and [j], are the three consonant glides of French. Some references prefer to call the glides semi-vowels.

To find the sound of [ɥ], sing the following examples. First, sustain the mixed vowel [y]. Then sing the word again, this time shortening the duration of the [y] until it becomes the glide [ɥ], a sound which is not sustained but moves quickly from one position to another.

A. Practice the French Glide [ɥ].

Sing these words to contrast the sounds [y] and [ɥ].

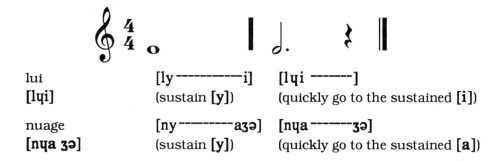

lui
[lɥi]

[ly----------i]
(sustain [y])

[lɥi ------]
(quickly go to the sustained [i])

nuage
[nɥa ʒə]

[ny---------aʒə]
(sustain [y])

[nɥa-------ʒə]
(quickly go to the sustained [a])

Read aloud these words using [ɥ].

lui	[lɥi]
nuage	[nɥaː ʒ]
bruit	[brɥi]
suis	[sɥi]
depuis	[də ˈpɥi]
fuyez	[fɥi je]
fuyant	[fɥi jɑ̃]
pluie	[plɥi]

The German "ch"

[ç]

[x]

The German "ch" [ç] and [x]

Forward "ch"

The IPA symbol [ç] is referred to as *forward ch*, as *ichlaut* [ɪçlaot], or simply by its sound. It is a voiceless palatal fricative consonant, made with the tip of the tongue behind the bottom front teeth, and the front of the tongue arched upward toward the hard palate at a point just behind the teeth ridge. The sound of *ichlaut* is similar to the sound of a whispered *ee* [i] or the sound of *h* in the English word *hue*.

The *ichlaut* [ç] sound occurs in several positions in German but mostly after forward vowels, mixed vowels or consonants as in *mich* [mɪç], *Bucher* [by çər], and *durch* [dʊrç].

A. Practice the German "ch" [ç].

Read aloud, to contrast the sounds of [ʃ] and [ç].

[ʃ] - [ç]   [ʃ] - [ç]   [ʃ] - [ç]

Read aloud these German words using *ichlaut* [ç].

dich	[dɪç]
licht	[lɪçt]
lieblich	['lip lɪç]
breche	[brɛ çə]
mich	[mɪç]
luftig	[lʊf tɪç]
sich	[zɪç]
mocht	[mœçt]
nicht	[nɪçt]
duftig	['dʊf tɪç]
Madchen	[mɛː tçən]
Gretchen	[grɛ tçən]
Der Erlkonig	[der 'ɛrl køː nɪç]
Veilchen	['fael çən]
euch	[ɔøç]
Vergebliches Standchen	[fɛr 'ge blɪ çəs ʃtɛn tçən]

The small mark at the bottom of [ç] *is called a cedille* [sə 'di jə]·

The *back "ch"* [x]

The IPA symbol [x], is referred to as *back ch*, as *achlaut* [xlaot], or simply by its sound. It is a voiceless velar fricative consonant made with the back of the tongue close to the soft palate (or velum) and the tip of the tongue behind the bottom front teeth. The exiting air makes a fricative sound, similar to a sharply whispered *ah* [ɑ]. An *achlaut* [x] occurs after a back vowel.

Read aloud, contrasting the sounds of [k] and [x].

[k] - [x]   [k] - [x]   [k] - [x]

Read aloud these German words using *achlaut* [x].

nach	[nax]
sucht	[zuxt]
Nacht	[naxt]
schwach	[ʃvax]
Bach	[bax]
ach	[ax]
Hauch	[haox]
gelacht	[gə'laxt]
auch	[aox]
Nachtigall	['nax ti gal]
noch	[nɔx]
Rache	[raxə]
kocht	[kɔxt]
vollbracht	['fɔl braxt]
Buch	[bux]
Strauch	[ʃtaox]

The German Diphthongs

The German Diphthongs

In German there are three diphthongs which correspond to diphthongs in English. Some texts use the same IPA symbols in German as in English, while other texts use a different IPA spelling for German.

In German the glides of the diphthongs are less forward than in English, giving a darker quality to the sounds of these vowels. The IPA symbols chosen for the glides in German reflect that difference. This text recommends the use of the German transcriptions listed below for the three diphthongs.

English	German
[aɪ] as in *might*	[ae] as in *Mai, meine*
[aʊ] as in *house*	[ao] as in *Augen*
[ɔɪ] as in *boy*	[ɔø] as in *Freude, Tannhäuser*

[ae]

[ao]

[ɔø]

A. Practice the German Diphthongs.

Read aloud these words using [ae].

sein	[zaen]
theilten	['tael tən]
meine	['mae nə]
dein	[daen]
eigen	['ae gən]
Saiten	['zae tən]
Schrei	[ʃrae]
einmal	['aen mal]

Read aloud these words using [ao].

Auge	['ao gə]
auf	[aof]
blaues	['blao əs]
gebaut	[gə 'baot]
traurig	['trao rɪç]
Laub	[laop]
lauter	['lao tər]
auch	[aox]

Read aloud these words using [ɔø].

neuen	['nɔø ən]
Freude	['frɔø də]
leuchtet	['lɔøç tət]
Streut	[ʃtrɔøt]
säuselt	['zɔø zəlt]
Fleuch	[flɔøç]
träumen	['trɔø mən]
euch	[ɔøç]

The Glottal Stop

The IPA symbol [ʔ] refers to a glottal stop, a voiceless plosive made by closing the vocal folds, building up breath pressure, and then suddenly opening the folds to release the breath plosively. The glottal stop occurs in German before stressed initial syllables beginning with a vowel. A glottal stop can be heard in English between words which end and begin with a vowel, as in *the apple* [ði ʔ 'æ pəl].

Some texts replace the [ʔ] with [|], an IPA symbol which indicates a pause. This text prefers [|] to indicate the glottal stop between words in German.

A. Practice the Glottal Stop.

Read aloud these sentences, using a glottal stop when indicated by [|].

Seit ich ihn gesehen   (Schumann)

[zaet | ɪç | iːn gəzeːən]

Du bist wie eine Blume   (Schumann)

[duː bɪst viː | aenə bluːmə]

Dies Bildnis ist bezaubernd schon   (Mozart)

[diːs bɪltnɪs | ɪst bətsaobərnt ʃøːn]

Dein blaues Auge   (Brahms)

[daen blaoəs | aogə]

Answer Sheets for Exercises

Chapter 4

page 22-B
1. [mi]
2. [min]
3. [kiz]
4. [pis]
5. [pis]
6. [piz]
7. [hi]
8. [fid]
9. [bist]
10. [fliz]
11. [flis]
12. [nit]
13. [ni]
14. [mit]
15. [wi]
16. [sid]
17. [lip]
18. [iv]
19. [bi]
20. [pip]
21. [li]
22. [pliz]

page 22-C
1. eat
2. deed
3. keen
4. heed
5. teak
6. seen
7. meal
8. team
9. free
10. cream

page 26-B
1. [hɪm]
2. ['wɪ mɪn]
3. [fin]
4. [mɪl]
5. [kɪdz]
6. [hɪz]
7. [kɪl]
8. [fɪz]
9. [dɪn]
10. [gɪgd]

1. [flɪt]
2. [gɪv]
3. [spik]
4. [mɪlk]
5. [mik]
6. [tɪnt]
7. [sɪt]
8. [mɪd]
9. ['bɪ lɪ]
10. ['lɪ lɪ]
11. [n 'siv]
12. [bɪ 'liv]
13. ['hɪ lɪ]
14. [tiz]

page 26-C
1. heat
2. hit
3. deep
4. dip
5. leave
6. live
7. seep
8. sip

page 32-C
1. [beɪlz]
2. [deɪl]
3. [weɪt]
4. [weɪt]
5. [eɪt]
6. [deɪn]
7. [veɪl]
8. [feɪl]
9. [beɪ]
10. [meɪ]
11. [feɪ]
12. [feɪn]
13. [greɪt]
14. [greɪt]
15. [greɪl]
16. [heɪl]

page 33-D
1. cape
2. mail
3. gay
4. vain
5. nape
6. pay
7. ace
8. vase
9. sane
10. state

page 33-E
1. [sil]
2. [rik]
3. [heɪ]
4. [keɪt]
5. [tik]
6. [ʊk]
7. [lɪd]
8. [keɪm]
9. [kɪs]
10. [si]
11. [vil]
12. [teɪl]

page 33-F
1. leak
2. lick
3. lake
4. meet
5. mitt
6. mate
7. pit
8. paid
9. deem
10. dim
11. date
12. mean
13. main
14. steed
15. stick
16. steak

page 39-B.
1. [sɛnt]
2. [bɛst]
3. [kɛlp]
4. [dɛnts]
5. [vɛt]
6. ['pɛ tɪ]
7. ['pɛ nɪ]
8. ['ɛ nɪ]
9. [gɛst]
10. [tɛmpts]
11. [blɛnd]
12. [bɛl]
13. [mɛt]
14. ['mɛ nɪ]

page 40-C
1. said
2. fell
3. help
4. elf
5. wed
6. end
7. bled
8. meant
9. left
10. Bess

page 40-D
1. [meɪld]
2. [eɪmd]
3. [ɛb]
4. [pik]
5. [nɛl]
6. [wɪn]
7. [wɛnd]
8. [weɪ]
9. [dɛt]
10. [deɪt]
11. [fɛld]
12. [pleɪd]
13. [stɪl]
14. [slɛd]
15. [nɪt]
16. [bɛlt]
17. [fɛɪd]
18. [fɛd]
19. [fɪt]
20. [fɪt]

page 40-E
1. gape
2. mill
3. geese
4. vail
5. let
6. day
7. deck
8. fist
9. game
10. step

page 44-B
1. [bæk]
2. [kæt]
3. [dæb]
4. [bæd]
5. [æks]
6. [pæd]
7. [ænt]
8. [ræt]
9. [læs]
10. [ædz]
11. [hæv]
12. [hæm]
13. [læm]
14. [kænt]
15. [hæk]
16. [blæk]

page 44-C
1. act
2. ham
3. rat
4. bran
5. tans
6. pack
7. tack
8. stamp

page 44-D
1. [læk]
2. [lik]
3. [seɪ]
4. [gɛt]
5. [hæt]
6. [pɛt]
7. [fæt]
8. [meɪn]
9. ['fi nɪks]
10. ['lɪ lɪ]
11. [gæs]
12. [lɪk]
13. [lɛt]
14. [tæb]
15. [geɪv]
16. [klæs]
17. [sɪt]
18. [mɪr]
19. [ræk]
20. [rɛk]

page 45
1. Texas
2. taxes
3. pest
4. past
5. lake
6. sand
7. blessed
8. bland
9. ski
10. live

Chapter 5

page 58-B
1. [bust]
2. [krud]
3. [sup]
4. ['ku ku]
5. [luk]
6. [spun]
7. [blu]
8. [tu]
9. [tu]
10. [grup]
11. [pruf]
12. [frut]
13. [nun]
14. [rud]
15. [kul]
16. [prun]

page 58-C
1. boon
2. tomb
3. lose
4. food
5. droop
6. clues
7. pool
8. brood
9. glue
10. mood

page 62-B
1. [bʊl]
2. [pʊt]
3. [kʊd]
4. [wʊlf]
5. [fʊt]
6. [wʊk]
7. [hʊk]
8. [bʊk]
9. [hʊd]
10. [wʊl]

page 62-C
1. [flu]
2. [fʊl]
3. [stʊl]
4. [stʊd]
5. [bʊm]
6. [luk]
7. [lʊk]
8. [wʊd]
9. [wʊd]
10. [mud]

page 62-D
1. prove
2. cook
3. soon
4. bull
5 pull
6. toots
7. book
8. groove

page 68-C
1. [goʊz]
2. [oʊn]
3. [koʊm]
4. [loʊn]
5. [noʊd]
6. [foʊ]
7. [moʊt]
8. [goʊt]
9. [loʊd]
10. [floʊt]

page 68-D
1. nose
2. soaks
3. mold
4. mode
5. mostly
6. boast

page 68-E
1. [koʊp]
2. [kul]
3. [koʊt]
4. [kuk]
5. [noʊn]
6. [noʊ]
7. [nun]
8. [nʊk]
9. [hoʊl]
10. [skroʊl]

page 69-F
1. could
2. lope
3. loon
4. stone
5. ooze
6. wood
7. boat
8. foot
9. coast
10. fool

page 72-B
1. [sɔ]
2. [vɔlt]
3. [kɔf]
4. [sɔt]
5. [bɔl]
6. [hɔrn]
7. [bɔt]
8. [kɔl]
9. [tɔt]
10. [stɔl]

page 72-C
1. law
2. pause
3. talk
4. ought
5. raw
6. coffin
7. office
8. salt

page 73-D
1. [krʊk]
2. [fɔlt]
3. [spun]
4. [nɔ]
5. [floʊ]
6. [lus]
7. [roʊm]
8. [wɔl]
9. [soʊ]
10. [flɔ]

page 73-E
1. home
2. loop
3. loft
4. look
5. tall
6. broad
7. grown
8. rude
9. bull
10. loaf

page 78-B
1. [kɑm]
2. [bɑm]
3. ['kwɑ lə tɪ]
4. [pɑm]
5. [pɑp]
6. [stɑp]
7. [gɑd]
8. [mɑp]
9. [mɑm]
10. [fɑnd]
11. [lɑk]
12. [sɑm]
13. [tɑp]
14. [rɑt]
15. [ɑ]
16. [spɑts]
17. [bɑm]
18. [dɑn]

page 78-C
1. cop
2. cod
3. hard
4. hock

Note: Several answers may have more than one correct spelling. For example, *wait* and *weight* will have the same IPA spelling.

223

Chapter 6

page 92-B
1. [pʌmp]
2. [lʌk]
3. [frʌm]
4. [dʌv]
5. [lʌv]
6. [kʌt]
7. [ʌp]
8. [sʌn]
9. [dʌg]
10. [kʌp]
11. [bʌdz]
12. [wʌn]
13. [wʌn]
14 [dʌst]

page 93-C
1. fund
2. rub
3. money
4. trucks
5. hum
6. buck
7. duck
8. buddy
9. stump
10. mud

page 96-B
1. [ˈbɑ təl]
2. [ˈsou dɪ əm]
3. [ə ˈdæpt]
4. [ə ˈfer]
5. [sə ˈpouz]
6. [ə ˈgen]
7. [kən ˈsɪs tənt]
8. [ˈɾʌ bəl]
9. [ˈɾʌm bəl]
10. [ˈprɛ zə dənt]
11. [ə ˈwer]
12. [ˈsɪm bəl]
13. [ə ˈdu]
14. [ˈbæ tə n̩]
15. [ˈmɪs tə n̩]
16. [ə ˈweɪ]
17. [ˈkæ mə rə]
18. [ˈkru əl]
19. [ˈkɑ mə]
20. [ˈpɪ rɪ əd]

page 96-C
1. double
2. secretary
3. adore
4. allophone
5. gallery
6. different
7. central
8. example
9. sudden
10. address
11. open
12. muffled

page 99-B
1. [ɝ k]
2. [ɝ n]
3. [fɝ]
4. [nɝ s]
5. [bɝ st]
6. [gɝ l]
7. [tɝ m]
8. [hɝ]
9. [sɝ]
10. [fɝ m]
11. [skɝ t]
12. [vɝ b]
13. [tɝ k]
14. [kɝ l]

page 99-C
1. lurk
2. curb
3. dirt
4. world
5. fur
6. purr
7. circle
8. word
9. perfect
10. fern
11. mercy
12. person
13. mermaid
14. fervid

page 101-B
1. [ˈsʌ fɚ]
2. [ˈfæk tɚ]
3. [pɪ lɚ]
4. [ˈdɑ lɚ]
5. [ˈfleɪ vɚ]
6. [ˈleɪ bɚ]
7. [ˈsep tɚ]
8. [ˈtræk tɚ]
9. [ˈmɪ vɚ]
10. [ˈsɝ fɚ]

page 101-C
1. [ˈlʌm bɚ]   [ˈlʌm bor]
2. [ˈrɛ rɚ]   [ˈrɛ ror]
3. [pɚ ˈmɪ tɪd]   [por ˈmɪ tɪd]
4. [ˈbe tɚ]   [ˈbe tor]
5. [ˈtrɛ mɚ]   [ˈtrɛ mor]
6. [pɚ ˈhæps]   [por ˈhæps]

page 101-D
1. skipper
2. patter
3. starter
4. perform
5. freezer
6. persist

page 104-B
1. [skwɝm]
2. [fɝm]
3. [lɝm]
4. [pɝrl]
5. [ˈwɝ n]
6. [ˈkɝ lɪ]
7. [kɝv]
8. [ˈfɝ lou]
9. [ˈkɝ dəl]
10. [spɝm]
11. [ˈgɝ dəl]
12. [tɝ bən]
13. [bɝr]
14. [lɝrk]
15. [lɝm]
16. [ˈɝm ɪst]
17. [hɝrl]
18. [ˈbɝr klɪ]
19 [pɝr]
20. [fɝrst]
21. [ˈhɝr dəl]
22. [ˈnɝr vəs]
23. [ˈtɝr təl]
24 [tɝr mɔɪl]

page 104-C
1. work
2. dirt
3. mercy
4. person
5. murder
6. surrey
7. perfect
8. survey
9. permanence
10. burn

Chapter 7

page 112-B
1. [traɪd]
2. [raɪd]
3. [aɪ]
4. [haɪ]
5. [aɪ ˈdi əz]
6. [faɪn]
7. [aɪs]
8. [raɪm]
9. [dɪ ˈnaɪ]
10. [klaɪd]
11. [haɪdz]
12. [ˈspaɪ dər]
13. [traɪ]
14 [laɪt]

page 112-C
1. describe
2. time
3. night
4. tide
5. prize
6. airline
7. Friday
8. brides
9. tribal
10. smile
11. might
12. idol
13. cry
14. guide

page 116-B
1. [gaʊn]
2. [ˈraʊ dɪ]
3. [ə ˈlaʊ]
4. [ə ˈnaʊns]
5. [ˈpraʊ lər]
6. [paʊt]
7. [ˈaʊn sɪz]
8. [faʊnd]
9. [plaʊ]
10. [braʊn]
11. [fraʊn]
12. [ˈmaʊn tən]
13. [aʊrz]
14 [ˈbaʊn də n̩]

page 116-C
1. round
2. brow
3. plowed
4. sound
5. trout
6. proud
7. cow
8. vowed
9. row
10. mound

page 120-B
1. [kɔ ɪ n]
2. [ˈɔɪnt mənt]
3. [hɔɪl]
4. [ˈrɔɪ əl]
5. [sɔɪl]
6. [ˈɔɪ lɪ]
7. [ˈfɔɪ bəlz]
8. [tɔɪ]
9. [brɔɪl]
10. [ˈɔɪs tər]
11. [ˈtɝr mɔɪl]
12. [ə ˈvɔɪd]
13. [n̩ ˈkɔɪl]
14. [ɪks ˈplɔɪ tɪd]

page 120-C
1. foil
2. poise
3. soiled
4. annoyed
5. hoist
6. coy
7. spoil
8. toys
9. adroit
10. toiled

page 124-B
1. [ˈjus fəl]
2. [ˈfju dəl]
3. [fjum]
4. [mjul]
5. [kju]
6. [mjut]
7. [ˈmju zɪ kəl]
8. [ju]
9. [ˈhju mə rəs]
10. [ˈbju tɪ]
11. [kjut]
12. [ju]
13. [ə ˈbju zɪz]
14. [kju mjə leɪt]

page 124-C
1. perfume
2. futile
3. pupil
4. puny
5. dual
6. fuse
7. accuse
8. union
9. unify
10. cue
11. pew
12. uniform
13. mew
14. mule

Chapter 9

page 136-B
1. [peg]
2. [beg]
3. [poul]
4. [boul]
5. [pen]
6. [ben]
7. [best]
8. [pest]
9. [bist]
10. [pis]

1. [ˈhæ pɪ]
2. [ˈæ bɪ]
3. [ˈpʌ pɪ]
4. [ˈbeɪ bɪ]
5. [ˈhelp fəl]
6. [ˈtrʌ bəl]
7. [ˈtʌm bəl]
8. [ˈtʌm pəl]
9. [ˈkeɪ pə bəl]
10. [ˈprʌ bə blɪ]

1. [ɪp]
2. [ɪb]
3. [kæp]
4. [kæb]
5. [mɑp]
6. [mɑb]
7. [sɑp]
8. [sɑb]
9. [roup]
10. [roub]

page 137-C
1. simple
2. symbol
3. ember
4. scamper
5. number
6. pamper
7. mapped
8. subsidize
9. optimum
10. grab

page 140-B
1. [tɔɪl]
2. [dɑn]
3. [daɪ]
4. [tɪn]
5. [dɪn]
6. [taɪ]
7. [toun]
8. [dun]

1. [ˈmɪ dəl]
2. [ə ˈteɪn]
3. [ˈmɪd ˌdeɪ]
4. [ˈsaʊn dɪd]
5. [ˈbe tər]
6. [ˈlæn təm]
7. [ˈnou tɪs]
8. [ˈmæn deɪt]

1. [send]
2. [sent]
3. [kɪkt]
4. [nʌt]
5. [nɑd]
6. [klɪpt]
7. [blɪd]
8. [hʌmd]

page 141-C
1. dud
2. debt
3. test
4. trek
5. dressed
6. bends
7. deadly
8. steep
9. dreads
10. addressed

page 144-B
1. [klæs]
2. [glæs]
3. [kraɪm]
4. [graɪm]
5. [keɪn]
6. [geɪn]

1. [ˈræ kɪt]
2. [ˈræ gɪd]
3. [wɪks]
4. [wɪgz]
5. [ˈæ ksə dənt]
6. [mɪks]

1. [pɪk]
2. [pɪg]
3. [lʌk]
4. [lʌg]
5. [æsk]
6. [mɔrg]

page 144-C
1. eggnog
2. lack
3. guest
4. kicks
5. kegs
6. glad
7. clipped
8. sixty
9. agreed
10. ugly

Chapter 10

page 150-B
1. [mi]
2. [mu]
3. [mʌst]
4. [mɑp]
5. [ˈmɛ n̩]
6. [maɪr]

1. [ˈhæ mər]
2. [ˈɑr mi]
3. [ˈsʌ mər]
4. [blumd]
5. [bleɪmd]
6. [ˈʊ mɪd]

1. [neɪm]
2. [aɪm]
3. [sʌm]
4. [sʌm]
5. [roum]
6. [tɪm]

page 150-C
1. slim
2. might
3. triumph
4. claim
5. common
6. music

4. extreme
5. tomb

page 154-B
1. [nout]   4. [neɪl]
2. [nɑk]   5. [nɪt]
3. [nɪp]   6. [naɪs]

1. ['bʌn dəl]   4. [ə 'nʌl]
2. ['te nər]   5. ['men təl]
3. [ɪn 'vent]   6. ['dou nər]

1. [mæn]   4. [braʊn]
2. [mun]   5. [stʌn]
3. [ɪn]   6. [fæn]

page 154-C
1. noose   6. translate
2. night   7. unlucky
3. undone   8. noon
4. rent   9. nifty
5. drained 10. untie

page158-B
1. [sɪŋ ər]   4. ['æŋ gjə lər]
2. ['mʌŋ kɪ]   5. ['strɔŋ lɪ]
3. [uŋ gəl]   6. ['læ rɪŋks]

1. [hʌŋ]   4. [sɔŋ]
2. [lɔŋ]   5. [ə 'mʌŋ]
3. [brɪŋ] 6. [rɪŋ]

page158-C
1. bang   6. swinger
2. rang   7. doing
3. brink   8. gang
4. sang   9. reading
5. tongs   10. wing

Chapter 11

page164-B
1. [fɪt]   4. [fæt]
2. [veɪl] 5. [væt]
3. [feɪl] 6. [vɪm]

1. [ə 'fer]   4. [n 'vɪl]
2. ['dɪf ər]   5. ['dræf tɪ]
3. ['le vər]   6. ['ou vər]

1. [reɪv]   4. [rɪf]
2. [kɔf]   5. [rʌf]
3. [stouv] 6. [self]

page164-C
1. half   6. calf
2. haves   7. defect
3. grief   8. loaf
4. grieves 9. loaves
5. fever   10. laughter

page 168-B
1. [ðiz]   4. [ðaɪn]
2. [θɪn]   5. [θɜrd]
3. [ðer]   6. [ðem]

1. ['ræ ðər]   4. ['fʌ ðər]
2. [me θəd]   5. ['we ðər]
3. ['ɛ θɪks]   6. [brɔθ]

1. [pæθ]   4. [breθ]
2. [raɪð]   5. [brɪð]
3. [bɪ 'niθ]   6. [suð]

page 168-C
1. this   6. seethe
2. three   7. month
3. lathe   8. wrath
4. myths   9. scathing
5. thimble 10. there

page 172-B
1. [soup]   5. [slɪp]
2. [zil]   6. [zum]
3. [sɪn]   7. [seɪn]
4. ['zi brə] 8. [zɪp]

1. ['pʌ zəl]   5. ['mju zɪk]
2. [ə 'bɪz məl] 6. ['frɪ zər]
3. ['mɪs tɪ]   7. ['θɜrs tɪ]
4. ['pen səl]   8. ['θɪ səl]

1. [rouz]   5. [ðiz]
2. [pæs]   6. [ðɪs]
3. [lægs]   7. [bets]
4. [pis]   8. [bedz]

page 172-C
1. sought   6. close
2. zone   7. close
3. zenith   8. cease
4. sound   9. sieze
5. diffuse   10. peas

page 176-B
1. [ʃi]
2. [ʃur]
3. [ʃip]

1. ['ou ʃən]   4. [dɪ 'lu ʒən]
2. ['fræk ʃən]   5. ['si ʒər]
3. [ə 'ʃur]   6. ['vɪ ʒu əl]

1. [mæʃ]   4. [beɪʒ]
2. [kæʃ]   5. [ruʒ]
3. [θræʃ]   6. [pres 'tiʒ]

page 176-C
1. rush   6. shame
2. shot   7. flesh
3. mirage   8. garage
4. occasion   9. vision
5. sugar   10. caution

page 179-B
1. [hit]   4. [houl]
2. [haʊnd]   5. ['hæ mər]
3. [hju]   6. [houm]

1. [ə 'hɛd]   4. [æn u 'his tə min]
2. [ˌʌn 'houl səm]   5. [ɪn 'hju mən]
3. [ɪn 'he rə təns]   6. [ʌp 'hɪl]

page 179-C
1. half   6. adhesive
2. hot   7. unhappy
3. haughty   8. heathen
4. hail   9. human
5. hug   10. beheaded

Chapter 12

page 184-B
1. [lɪt]   4. [lɪm]
2. [lɪp]   5. [lɪf]
3. [luz]   6. ['lɪ vər]

1. ['wel θɪ]   4. ['de lə kət]
2. ['pul pɪt]   5. [ʃoul dər]
3. ['sʌl kɪ]   6. ['sel ɪŋ]

1. ['fʌ nəl]   4. ['pɑr pəl]
2. ['mɪ dəl]   5. ['kæ təl]
3. [n 'kɔl]   6. ['ou pəl]

page 184-C
1. miller   6. vile
2. all   7. ceiling
3. sailor   8. lame
4. already   9. lid
5. calender   10. bowl

Chapter 13

page 190-B
1. [rouz]   5. [rekt]
2. [red]   6. [raɪt]
3. [reɪl]   7. [rɔ]
4. [ril]   8. [reɪt]

1. [ə 'graʊnd]   5. [ə 'rest]
2. [ɪ 'roud]   6. [traɪt]

3. ['ve n]   7. [θri]
4. [ʌp 'rut]   8. [ə 'raɪ]

1. [kar]   5. [four]
2. [fɪr]   6. [per]
3. [pɑr]   7. [per]
4. [tur]   8. [dɪr]

page 190-C
1. reason   6. furious
2. reef   7. carry
3. friend   8. freely
4. bring   9. rights
5. mystery   10. more

page 194-B
1. [jild]   4. ['ju nə ˌfaɪd]
2. [jæm]   5. ['ju sɪʤ]
3. [juθ]   6. ['jes tər ˌdeɪ]

1. ['pɪn jən]   4. [sə 'vɪl jən]
2. ['jun jən]   5. ['kæn jən]
3. ['bɪl jən]   6. ['wɪl jəm]

page 194-C
1. trillion   5. yoga
2. yet   6. yank
3. yellow   7. yeast
4. unite   8. year

page 198-B
1. [hwɜrld]   [wɜrld]
2. [hweɪl]   [weɪl]
3. ['hwɪ ðər]   ['wɪ ðər]
4. [hwit]   [wi]
5. [hwaɪl]   [waɪl]
6. [hwɜrd]   [wɜrd]
7. [hwaɪn]   [waɪn]
8. ['hwɪs pər] [wɪsp]
9. [hwet]   [wet]
10. [hwaɪt]   [waɪld]

1. [swæg]   5. [kwɪt]
2. [dwel]   6. [kweɪl]
3. [twen tɪ] 7. [kwɪk]
4. [dwɔrf]   8. [kwaɪr]

page 198-C
1. whale   6. quail
2. way   7. swallow
3. whistle   8. walnut
4. wine   9. whirl
5. quill   10. were

Chapter 13

page204-B
1. [ʤɪl]   6. ['ʤen təl]
2. [ʤɪl]   7. [tʃʌmp]
3. [tʃest]   8. [ʤʌmp]
4. [ʤest]   9. [tʃɪp]
5. [tʃɪn]   10. [ʤɪn]

1. ['ɛtʃ ɪŋ]   6. ['ri ʤənt]
2. ['ɛʤ ɪŋ]   7. ['lʌn tʃɪz]
3. ['sɑrtʃ ɪŋ] 8. ['lʌn ʤɪz]
4. ['sɜrʤ ɪŋ]   9. ['ke tʃəp]
5. ['rɪtʃ ɪst] 10. ['mɪ ʤət]

1. [liʧ]   6. [grʌʤ]
2. [leʤ]   7. [krʌtʃ]
3. [pɑrtʃ]   8. [streɪnʤ]
4. [pɑrʤ]   9. [tʃɜrtʃ]
5. [hætʃ]   10. [ʤʌʤ]

page204-C
1. children   6. juice
2. gem   7. hatchet
3. suggest   8. jail
4. ritual   9. perjury
5. cellist   10. virtue

Acknowledgments

I would like to express my deep appreciation to several colleagues and friends for their enthusiasm and untiring help in the production of this book. I am grateful to Bobbie Caldwell for her amazing all around help, to Karen Kelsey for her sharp eyes and ears and hours of cheerful proofreading, and to Cheryl Golden for her help in proofing the manuscript.

Special thanks goes to my husband, Ernest Ludwick, whose artistic talent produced the diagrams and drawings for the text and whose constant patience offers such loving support.

Finally, heartfelt thanks to my publisher and editor, Robert Caldwell, who kept the inspiration flowing.

Of interest from Pst...Inc

IPA Wall Mount Symbols 30.00 (with Consonants, 50.00)
Color-coded, one symbol per 8 1/2 by 11 page, laminated IPA Symbols for use in the classroom.

Diction for Singers
A concise reference for English, Italian, Latin, German, French, and Spanish pronunciation.
Wall, Caldwell, Gavilanes, Allen 29.95

"...found Diction for Singers to be clear and creative, especially with the use of the IPA symbols. The book is exactly right for those of us who are in the situation of having to teach a crash course for one year. In fact, I find it even better than that. It can be used for longer periods and now I don't have to compile many resources." *Laury Christy, University of South Carolina*

"Finally a book tailor-made for the diction classroom, one that does not force the teacher to supplement from other texts. This book is very well organized and easy to understand. It is also an excellent reference for any singer or teacher of singing." *Ann Harrell, Hardin-Simmons University*

The Performer Prepares
Robert Caldwell 16.95

"I don't know of another book of its kind. It is well researched, well-meant, and deserves recognition and a lot of attention.... The Performer Prepares can and should be of definite help to many musicians who either aspire to perform or having started to appear on stage need help, be it of psychological or just simply practical nature. " *Vladimir Ashkenazy*

"(Caldwell) has carefully laid out a map for traveling a treacherous road. ...we are provided with a unique hands-on approach to the subjective aspects of (performing) charisma, presence, nerves, stage fright, tension, and conviction. This book is recommended as a useful resource for students and professionals." *The American Music Teacher*

"I was in a piano recital in seventh grade and that's as close as I've ever gotten—or ever wanted to get—to giving a performance. And while, like most people, I believe that I can "recognize" a "great performance" when I see or hear one, I have no idea what it takes to be a great performer. Robert Caldwell addresses this issue in The Performer Prepares. ...Rather than follow a vague admonition "be more creative," his new book discusses several practical techniques to develop imagination so that it is in line with the performer's personality." *The Discriminating Librarian*

Studio Manger for Professional Musicians
Full featured software for managing Students, Repertoire, Performances, Inventory, Income, and Expenses.

You may order any of the items above, The Professional Singer's Bookshelf Catalogue, and additional copies of IPA for Singers directly from the publisher:

Pst...Inc
P.O. Box 800208H
Dallas, Tx 75380-0208